THE JAMES SPRUNT STUDIES IN HISTORY AND POLITICAL SCIENCE

*Published under the Direction of
the Departments of History and Political Science
of the University of North Carolina*

VOLUME 34

———————— * ————————

Editors

FLETCHER M. GREEN
WILLIAM WHATLEY PIERSON
MITCHELL B. GARRETT
KEENER C. FRAZER
J. CARLYLE SITTERSON

THE POLITICAL LIBERALISM OF
THE NEW YORK *NATION*
1865-1932

By

ALAN PENDLETON GRIMES

Associate Professor of Political Science
Michigan State College

CHAPEL HILL

———— ✱ ————

THE UNIVERSITY OF NORTH CAROLINA PRESS

1953

Copyright, 1953, by
THE UNIVERSITY OF NORTH CAROLINA PRESS

INTRODUCTION

American periodical literature as a source of influential political ideas is a field still largely unexplored by political scientists. Yet the editors of periodicals have contributed to the shaping of American thought. In the periodical field the function of relaying information becomes joined with the function of interpreting the news. Thus, over a period of time the faithful reader encounters a fairly rounded out system of political thought, which, though it lacks the inner consistency of a formal treatise, nevertheless presents an attitude toward political questions and, in a democracy, may be not only influential but vitally consequential. Like the author of a political treatise the editor of a periodical must base his judgments of political issues on some standard, implicit or expressed. The author, however, has an advantage over the editor, for he may work removed from the press of time. The editor lives in a world of immediate political issues upon which he must pass judgment prior to a deadline. Still, the editor has the advantage over the author; he deals with issues while they are crucial and alive. Thus his decisions may have an immediate effect upon governmental policy. The author of a treatise must deal, by and large, in generalities and trust in the reader's fidelity to his standard for the settlement of subsequent particular political problems. The editor, dealing with present politics rather than history, with contemporary personalities rather than past heroes, with rights endangered and wrongs to be rectified, with the whole machinery of government in motion, writes of the excitement and vibrancy of history in the making, and his periodical may become not only a source of history but one of its makers. In all certainty, the files of an influential periodical where there has been longevity and sufficient continuity of editorial policy reflect at least one segment of American political thought.

Such a journal is the New York *Nation*. Founded in 1865, it possesses longevity, influence, and a rare consistency in editorial policy over long periods of time. It is this longevity, constancy, and influence which make *The Nation*, within given periods of time, not unlike a consequential political treatise and, therefore, a fit subject for study in the development of American political thought. Its standard of judgment throughout all its history has been its conception of that congeries of ideas commonly referred to as "liberalism." Even today it prides itself on being "America's Leading Liberal Weekly since 1865." Thus one may catch some gleam of the meaning of liberalism in America by examining *The Nation's* files from 1865 to 1932. The year 1932 is a convenient place to end this study because in that year a change of editors coincided with the advent of the New Deal and the triumph, at least temporarily, of progressivism in American politics.

As the organ through which many recognized leaders of liberalism chose to express their views on contemporaneous affairs, *The Nation's* influence has far exceeded its circulation. *The Nation* started with a circulation of 5,000 readers and continued through the turn of the century with a circulation generally under 10,000. By 1916, the circulation ran to over 15,000 and by 1928, exceeded 40,000.[1] But its subscribers have always included libraries, universities, and other educational centers throughout the country, just as its contributors—from Albert Dicey to Harold Laski, from James Bryce to Ramsay MacDonald, from James Russell Lowell to Raymond Gram Swing, from William Graham Sumner to Stuart Chase, from Francis Lieber to Freda Kirchwey—have always included the educated leaders who sway opinion. For many years it was the policy of *The Nation* to publish only unsigned articles so that the reader was unaware of the identity of the contributors save for an occasional advertisement listing well over a hundred distinguished men of letters. This practice, however, was discontinued after the first World War.

When, in 1875, Richard Henry Dana, Jr. wrote to his son who was preparing to travel abroad that he would forward to him the New York *Nation* ("They will keep you well up in American affairs."), he was expressing the confidence which men in his class had in that magazine.[2] *The Nation* was, in the opinion of Lord Bryce, "the best weekly not only in America but in the world." "It was read," Bryce noted, "by the two classes which in America have most to do with forming political and economic opinion—I mean editors and University teachers."[3] A biographer of Theodore Roosevelt found that the editor of the late nineteenth-century *Nation* "was one of the critics who rarely failed to penetrate Roosevelt's gradually thickening hide."[4] By 1923, there were, fashioned after the New York *Nation*, *Die Nation* in Berlin, the London *Nation*,[5] a Canadian *Nation*, a Mexican *Nation*, and even a *Nation* in Lahore, India.[6]

[1] *The Nation*, CI (1915), 53; CII (1916), 88; CXXVII (1928), 699.
[2] Richard H. Dana, III (ed.), *Richard Henry Dana, Jr.* (Boston: Houghton, Mifflin Company, 1910), p. 487.
[3] James Bryce, *Studies in Contemporary Biography* (New York: The Macmillan Company, 1903), pp. 372, 378.
[4] Henry F. Pringle, *Theodore Roosevelt* (New York: Harcourt, Brace and Company, 1931), p. 33.
[5] Since 1931 *The New Statesman and Nation*.
[6] In 1939, many liberals could agree with the judgment of Professor Thurman Arnold regarding the place of *The Nation* (and *The New Republic*) in American thought. "I can tell what my liberal colleagues are going to say tomorrow by reading articles in these two publications to-day. In this country, periodical literature has been more important than books and there have been more new notions put across by these two publications than any other two in the history of American letters." Cited in Malcolm Cowley and Bernard Smith, *Books That Changed Our Minds* (New York: Doubleday, Doran and Company, Inc., 1939), pp. 8-9.

INTRODUCTION

A large share of the credit for the prestige of *The Nation* in American thought must go to Edwin Lawrence Godkin, its founder and first editor. Born in Ireland of English parents in 1831, he received a thorough education, taking his degree at Queen's College, Belfast. Early fired with the cause of democracy, he wrote a history of Hungary when only twenty-two to popularize the struggles of Kossuth. As a correspondent for the London *Daily News* he served in the Crimea, and in 1856 came to the United States. After a tour of the Southern states, he settled in New York and studied law. Reading in the office of David Dudley Field, he was admitted to the New York bar in 1858. However, his real interests were politics and journalism.

In 1865 Godkin's ambition to found and edit a non-partisan weekly materialized. James Miller McKim, wealthy Philadelphia abolitionist, who was interested in establishing a paper to support the cause of the freedmen, raised the greater part of the necessary funds, and Godkin's friend, Charles Eliot Norton, contributed heavily to this venture. On July 6, 1865, the first issue of *The Nation* appeared, with Edwin Lawrence Godkin as editor and Wendell Phillips Garrison, son of the noted abolitionist and son-in-law of McKim, as literary editor. Thus was formed the editorial team that was to last till the end of the century.

A publisher's prospectus announcing the birth of *The Nation* listed seven main objectives, of which three were concerned with the elevation of the freedmen in the South. The other objects included the accurate discussion of public affairs, the diffusion of democratic principles, an emphasis on the importance of public education and art and literary criticism. "*The Nation* will not be the organ of any party, sect, or body" the prospectus added.[7] While the emphasis on these objects has varied with editors, *The Nation* has remained consistently faithful to its announced standard of political independence. An early *Nation* editorial declared:

Our criticisms . . . may be ill-founded or ill-judged, but are always honest, and they shall certainly never be withheld; they shall go before our readers, like testimony before the courts, for what they are worth.[8]

The Nation proposed to bring to its readers the best thoughts of the best minds, and in this endeavor it has been largely successful. Henry Holt wrote in 1915 that Godkin of *The Nation* had been "an authority with authorities."[9] When Godkin died in 1902, Charles Eliot Norton wrote:

He did more than any other writer of his generation to clarify the intelligence and to quicken the conscience of the thoughtful part of the community in regard to every important political question of the time.[10]

[7] Rollo Ogden (ed.), *Life and Letters of Edwin Lawrence Godkin* (New York: The Macmillan Company, 1907), I, 237-238.
[8] *The Nation*, II (1866), 166.
[9] *Ibid.*, CI (1915), 48.
[10] Charles Eliot Norton, *Letters of Charles Eliot Norton* (Boston: Houghton, Mifflin Company, 1913), II, 323.

The philosopher, William James, paid a similar tribute to Godkin:

> To my generation, his was certainly the towering influence in all thought concerning public affairs, and indirectly his influence has certainly been more pervasive than that of any other writer of the generation, for he influenced other writers who never quoted him, and determined the whole current of discussion.[11]

In 1881, Henry Villard, the rising railroad magnate[12] (and W. P. Garrison's brother-in-law), purchased the New York *Evening Post*, and Godkin joined the *Evening Post* as associate editor. *The Nation*, sold to the proprietors of the *Evening Post*, became in a large measure the *Post's* weekly edition. Thus, in the main, the political articles that appeared in *The Nation* had previously appeared in the *Evening Post*. Garrison continued as editor of *The Nation*, but in reality most of its articles came from the pen of E. L. Godkin, who in 1883 became editor-in-chief of the *Evening Post*.

In 1900 Godkin retired from the *Evening Post* and was succeeded by Horace White, while Garrison remained as *The Nation's* editor until 1906. Rollo Ogden became editor of the *Evening Post* in 1903 and continued in this capacity until 1920. "The earlier years of *The Nation* were its best," Oswald Garrison Villard has written.

> After it became affiliated with the *Evening Post* in 1881 it lost much of its spontaneity and under Wendell Phillips Garrison's influence . . . it became less and less polemical and more and more the organ of an intense scholarship. . . .[13]

In 1906 Hammond Lamont, brother of the wealthy financier, became editor of *The Nation*. Like Garrison, he had been educated at Harvard. He had worked on newspapers, taught English at Harvard and rhetoric at Brown, and been managing editor of the *Evening Post* prior to assuming the editorship of *The Nation*. However, his career was cut short by his untimely death in 1909.

Paul Elmer More succeeded Lamont. More held an A.M. from Harvard at which University he taught Sanscrit prior to joining the *Evening Post* as literary editor in 1904. He left *The Nation* in 1914 to teach at Princeton University, and Harold de Wolf Fuller became editor. Fuller took his A.B., A.M., and Ph.D. at Harvard where he taught English prior to becoming assistant editor of *The Nation* in 1911. In January, 1918, Oswald Garrison Villard took over the editorship of *The Nation* and in July of that year sold the New York *Evening Post*

---

[11] Cited in Ogden, *op. cit.*, I, 221.
[12] It should be noted that *The Nation's* conservative attitude toward government regulation of the railroads (*infra*, Chapter II, pp. 27-29) does not reflect the Villard purchase as *The Nation* had taken this stand on the railroads at least ten years earlier.
[13] *The Nation*, CXXI (1925), 8.

so that once again *The Nation* and the *Evening Post* went their separate ways. Villard retained the active editorship of *The Nation* until 1932.

The Nation, under the editorships of Lamont, More, and Fuller, lost a good deal of the verve and flavor it had possessed under Godkin and was to regain under Villard. Lamont, More, and Fuller were as much academicians as journalists and their work reveals more of an earnest scholarship than a zest for contemporary political life. Villard, also educated at Harvard, where he taught American history from 1894 to 1896, returned to *The Nation* its former crusader's zeal. William Hard wrote that Villard "made more acres of public men acutely miserable, per unit of circulation, than any other editor alive."[14] Under Villard, *The Nation* advertised itself as "the foremost exponent of uncompromising liberalism in America."[15] In 1928, Karl A. Bickel, then president of the United Press, declared that Villard's *Nation* was "The best obtainable barometer on the state of liberal opinion in the United States."[16]

The Nation's sixty-seven years, from its commencement by Godkin in 1865 to the relinquishment of the editorship by Villard in 1932, reveal the progress of a vital segment of American thought. Pitched more for educated readers than for the masses, *The Nation* has in part reflected, in part stimulated, but without doubt influenced the political thinking of America. Within the years 1865-1932 Americans were faced with the readjustment of their historic ideals to the political and economic realities of a mammoth industrial development. This process of readjustment is in part evidenced by the transition in American liberal thought from the old liberalism to the new. Because socialism, as a formal doctrine, has never seemed acceptable to most American liberals, it has been omitted from this study. As may be seen in the following pages, however, democratic liberalism has adopted, in its own fashion, no little of the content of socialistic thought. The development of American liberalism since 1865 has not been a systematic process but rather one that has proceeded with mighty spurts and occasional retrogressions. No better portrayal of this movement, with its high ideals and frequent flaws, may be had than in the files of *The Nation* magazine.

A survey of this nature has made necessary considerable selectivity. Thus minor contradictions and certain subject matter have been excluded in an effort to preserve the general trend of thought. The study itself is the outgrowth of an idea developed by Dr. Charles B. Robson in one of his seminars in American political thought at the University of North Carolina. With patient encouragement and stimulating discussion, he was of inestimable assistance to the writer in carrying this project forward to its completion.

[14] *Ibid.*, CL (1940), 158.
[15] *Ibid.*, CIX (1919), 536.
[16] *Ibid.*, CXXVII (1938), ii facing p. 53.

CONTENTS

	PAGE
Introduction	v
I. The Evanescent Triumph of American Democracy	3
II. Liberal Political Economy	13
III. Respectable Reform	36
IV. Progressivism: The Union of Politics and Economics	55
V. Little America and Pacifist Liberalism	71
VI. The Triumph of Business Politics	93
VII. The Progressive Course of Liberalism	111
Bibliography	123
Index	131

THE POLITICAL LIBERALISM OF
THE NEW YORK *NATION*
1865-1932

CHAPTER I

THE EVANESCENT TRIUMPH OF AMERICAN DEMOCRACY*

To contemporary liberals the American Civil War was more than a sectional conflict concerned with the preservation of the Union or the continuance of slavery. It was a struggle between oligarchic privilege and democratic enlightenment. Although the American experiment in democracy had successfully resisted its external enemies, it now appeared in danger of collapsing from internal dissension, thus fulfilling the dire expectations of its hostile critics. Europe as well as America felt that the outcome would have tremendous implications for the course of future democratic practice. John Bright, champion of English liberalism, addressed the Trade Unions of London in 1863 on the import of the war. "Privilege," he declared, "has shuddered at what might happen to old Europe if this grand experiment [the American Republic] should succeed."[1] As an English commentator later remarked, "If democracy triumphed in America, nothing could long delay its advent here."[2]

Because the issues involved were of such great concern, Lee's surrender was hailed by the liberals as a turning point in the history of democracy. The Republic had survived the bloodiest conflict of the century and, with slavery abolished, the path seemed clear to the liberal democratic ideals of peace, progress, and reform, culminating in a free society composed of free men of all races. From France, John Stuart Mill wrote optimistically to one of his disciples, E. L. Godkin, "The great concussion which has taken place in the American mind must have loosened the foundations of all prejudices and secured a fair hearing for impartial reason on all subjects such as it might not otherwise have had for many generations."[3]

In England, Bright noted in his private journal: "This great triumph of the Republic is the event of our age. The friends of freedom everywhere should thank God and take courage."[4] In Boston, Richard Henry Dana, Jr., sailor and jurist, boasted to a cheering audience, "For the first time in history, a self-governing republic is capable of maintaining

* The latter half of this chapter has previously been published in the *Bulletin of Negro History*, Vol. XIV, Dec. 1950, under the title "Negro Suffrage and Nineteenth Century Liberalism: Views of the New York *Nation* During Reconstruction." Permission has been granted by the editors for its use here.
[1] George Macauley Trevelyan, *The Life of John Bright* (London: Constable and Company, Ltd., 1925), p. 307.
[2] *Ibid.*, p. 304.
[3] Hugh S. R. Elliot (ed.), *The Letters of John Stuart Mill* (London: Longmans, Green and Co., 1910), II, 36.
[4] Trevelyan, *op. cit.*, p. 325.

itself against internal rebellion."[5] The war had been fought, wrote James Russell Lowell, "to save the experiment of democracy from destruction,"[6] and the victory had proven to the Old World "the amazing strength and no less amazing steadiness of democratic institutions."[7] Harvard held a Commemoration service at which Lowell recited his "Commemoration Ode": "O Beautiful! my Country! ours once more!"[8] George William Curtis concluded his popular speech entitled "The Good Fight" with this glowing forecast: "For our America shall be the Sinai of the nations, and from the terrible thunders and lightnings of its great struggle shall proceed the divine law of liberty that shall subdue and harmonize the world."[9]

So high ran the tide of democratic optimism that William Lloyd Garrison, fiery editor of the *Liberator*, could write, "At last, the old 'covenant with death' is annulled, and the 'agreement with hell' no longer stands."[10] Finding that the object of the *Liberator* had been "consummated," Garrison, with one last invocation to the "Spirit of Freedom," ceased publication.[11]

Amidst this general rejoicing, a staunch young liberal, Edwin Lawrence Godkin, founded *The Nation* magazine. In the first issue, which happily coincided with the Fourth of July celebrations of 1865, *The Nation*, writing on the "triumph of American democracy," declared:

We utter no idle boast when we say that if the conflict of ages, the great strife between the few and the many, between privilege and equality, between law and power, between opinion and the sword, was not closed on the day on which Lee threw down his arms, the issue was placed beyond doubt.[12]

In 1865 democracy was no longer a vision but a reality to intellectual liberals, who glorying in the triumph of their democratic faith, turned confidently to the future.

The selection of "The Nation" as a title for a New York magazine is suggestive. The Civil War had been over but a few months when the idea that the process of preserving the Union had, in fact, given birth to the American nation became apparent. Even the shibboleth "Union," the victorious rallying cry, began to slip out of common parlance and into a special usage reserved for political conventions, as men and women began to think and act in terms of a nation composed

[5] Catherine Drinker Bowen, *Yankee from Olympus* (Boston: Little, Brown, and Company, 1944), p. 212.
[6] James Russell Lowell, *Works* (Boston: Houghton, Mifflin and Company, 1888), V, 217.
[7] *Ibid.*, p. 210.
[8] *Ibid.*, IV, 31.
[9] Charles E. Norton, *Orations and Addresses of George William Curtis* (New York: Harper and Brothers, 1894), I, 177.
[10] W. P. Garrison and F. J. Garrison, *William Lloyd Garrison, The Story of His Life, Told by His Children* (New York: The Century Co., 1889), IV, 167.
[11] *Ibid.*, pp. 173-174.
[12] *The Nation*, I (1865), 5.

of the people as a whole, rather than of thirty-six federated units. "The tendency of the modern period of society . . . is toward nationalization," *The Nation* observed, "and against either a feudal federation or a despotic centralization."[13] The American nation, composed of a sovereign people possessing a common heritage, jealous of their personal rights, rights which were protected by the institutions of local self-government, had achieved something which marked a new era in the history of political thought:

Sovereignty without centralization, consolidation without despotism, nationality under democratic forms, this is a fact now for the first time established in the history of government.[14]

The new nation, built upon the old, was the post-war synthesis of pre-war nationalism and particularism. Before it now lay the gigantic task of reconstruction and the practical application of democratic principles.

The practical application of democratic principles to the specific problems of reconstruction soon brought about a schism in the liberal ranks. "The first question that arises in the mind of everybody in thinking of reconstruction is," Lowell observed, "What is to be done about the negro?"[15] Here was the basic issue which eventually was to set the President against Congress, Congress against the Court, and liberal against radical. Since the war had been fought to preserve the democratic experiment, "and put it in a fairer way of success by removing the single disturbing element,"[16] it was now imperative to take some positive steps toward achieving for the Negro that measure of equality without which democracy would be incomplete. For if the war had proved, as Lowell held, "the everlasting validity of the theory of the Declaration of Independence,"[17] the immediate problem at hand was to put this theory into practice in the South.

To *The Nation* the idea of equality affirmed in the Declaration of Independence meant

the equal right of all to attain that which is made attainable to any . . . the equal right of every man that the law should lay nothing in his way to the becoming possessed of such franchises, suffrage, or political privileges of any kind that is not also laid in the way of every other man, or that there should be nothing removed from the path of any other man that is not, so far as the law is concerned, also taken out of his.[18]

In order to make possible this equality for the Negro, it endorsed the early Reconstruction program: the Freedmen's Bureau, the Civil Rights bill of 1866, the reconstruction acts of 1867, and the war amendments. It took issue with Henry Ward Beecher and the others who in preference

[13] *Ibid.*, p. 38.
[15] Lowell, *op. cit.*, V, 223.
[17] *Ibid.*, p. 256.
[14] *Ibid.*, p. 39.
[16] *Ibid.*, p. 217.
[18] *The Nation*, I (1865), 72.

to the reconstruction measures would leave the Negro's future condition up to the general laws of progress and acts of Providence. Positive government interference was required.

> A government which tells a citizen or subject who complains to it that he is oppressed or mutilated by his fellow-citizens, as Mr. Beecher wants our Government to tell the Southern freedmen, that he must look for an improvement in his condition to the general progress of Southern society, absolves him from his allegiance.[19]

It favored whatever use of force might be necessary in order to protect the Southern Negro, and, thus, would not hasten to receive the South back in the Union. "The South," it noted, "will never be really in this Union until Henry Ward Beecher can read an article from the New York *Tribune* on the steps of the principal hotel in Jackson, Mississippi . . ." without fear of harm.[20]

Charles Sumner resolved the constitutional difficulty of reconstruction with the sweeping assertion that "Whatever you enact for Human Rights is Constitutional."[21] While *The Nation* would not subscribe to so loose a view of the Constitution, it did feel that while Congress was legislating for the Negro the courts should not interfere with the program. It believed in a "strict adherence to the Constitution, but not a strict construction of it."[22] Since reconstruction was supported by a majority of the people, it should not be hampered by judicial restraint. "All devices for protection against the will of a decided majority of the governing class are certain to fail," *The Nation* declared, "and nothing is more unwise than to thrust a few judges across the path which such a majority have resolved to pursue."[23] At another time *The Nation* noted that "The Constitution . . . cannot have any more force than the majority gives it."[24] For the courts to rule on reconstruction would be nothing but a "political act," in fact, it would be "legislation." "Clothing it in the form of a judicial decision would not alter its character."[25] Without judicial interference, the Negro must be educated to and protected in his new equal status in the new society.

Basically, however, *The Nation's* program was a moderate one, far more cautious than that of the Committee of Fifteen, and its optimism was far more temperate than that of the radical reformers. For, it prudently observed, "anybody who expects Southern whites and blacks to settle down into their true and just relations to each other without breaking one another's heads a good deal, knows little either of history or human nature."[26]

At the heart of the question of equality stood the problem of Negro suffrage. John Stuart Mill had written to Parke Godwin shortly after

[19] *Ibid.*, III (1866), 231.
[20] *Ibid.*, II (1865), 70.
[21] Charles Sumner, *Works* (Boston: Lee and Shepard, 1883), XIII, 38.
[22] *The Nation*, IV (1867), 254.
[23] *Ibid.*, p. 394.
[24] *Ibid.*, V (1868), 210.
[25] *Ibid.*, VI (1868), 44.
[26] *Ibid.*, I (1865), 616.

the war endorsing "full equality of political rights to negroes."[27] Lowell enquired, "Must we not make them voters also, that they may have that power of self-protection which no interference of government can so safely, cheaply, and surely exercise in their behalf?"[28] In Boston's Faneuil Hall, Richard Henry Dana, Jr., reminded his audience that "Our covenant with the freedmen is sealed in blood!" and declared, "To introduce the free negroes to the voting franchise is a revolution. *If we do not secure that now, in the time of revolution, it can never be secured, except by a new revolution.*"[29] Charles Sumner, militant champion of Negro suffrage, addressed his fellow Senators:

To him who has the ballot, all other things shall be given—protection, opportunity, education, a homestead. The ballot is the Horn of Abundance, out of which overflow rights of every kind, with corn, cotton, rice, and all the fruits of the earth.[30]

Speaking in Philadelphia, Carl Schurz declared: "I believe that to place the government of the late rebel States upon a reliable loyal foundation, you must enfranchise all the loyal men, black as well as white...." Furthermore, he noted that "the development of free labor and the cause of democratic government requires the enfranchisement of the negro just as much as the negro needs it for his own protection."[31] Wendell Phillips stated, "The black man without the ballot, is the lamb given over to the wolf."[32]

Thus to many of the liberal group, true equality and sound reconstruction required the franchise for the Negro. *The Nation*, however, approached the question of Negro suffrage much more cautiously. Unlike Lowell and Sumner, it saw no basis whatsoever for the alleged natural right of the Negro or anyone else to vote.[33] A state might set whatever qualifications for suffrage that it saw fit; in fact, "a wise state *should* demand conditions."[34] But these conditions should be such that any individual, through his own efforts, might attain the requisite qualifications.

Prior to the conclusion of the war, Godkin, in a letter to Charles Eliot Norton, had pointed out that "there is no natural right to share in the government" for that determination must be made by the state. Furthermore, he observed, popular acceptance of the natural right theory

---

[27] Elliot, *op. cit.*, p. 33.
[28] Lowell, *op. cit.*, V, 228.
[29] Richard H. Dana, III (ed.), *Richard Henry Dana, Jr.* (Boston: Houghton, Mifflin Company, 1910), pp. 250-251.
[30] Sumner, *op. cit.*, X, 223-224.
[31] Frederic Bancroft, *Speeches, Correspondence, and Political Papers of Carl Schurz* (New York: G. P. Putnam's Sons, 1913), I, 403.
[32] *Anti-Slavery Standard*, Vol. XXX, No. 3, cited in Carlos Martyn, *Wendell Phillips* (New York: Funk & Wagnalls, 1890), p. 363.
[33] *The Nation*, III (1866), 497.
[34] *Ibid.*, I (1865), 74.

would be likely to have an unfortunate effect as it would tend "to lessen or destroy the feeling of responsibility necessary to a proper exercise of the suffrage, especially amongst ignorant voters." The natural right theory, he advised Norton, was "a positive and powerful obstacle to the establishment even of that educational test which you acknowledge to be necessary to the security of a government resting on the intelligence of the people."[35]

The guarantee of a republican form of government was no ground for extending the franchise, *The Nation* pointed out to Congress. For until the Civil War we had accepted slavery and disfranchisement under the republican form.[36] Nor did democracy itself demand universal suffrage. Many people, it observed, confused the two terms, and some, indeed, believed they were synonymous. The fact that a broad suffrage often existed in a democracy had had a misleading effect. It had caused some to claim that in a country where a large percentage of the people were disfranchised, democracy did not exist and that where the people enjoyed an extended franchise, there, *ipso facto*, must be democracy. By way of disproving this, *The Nation* pointed to Athens, as perhaps the most famous democracy, which had had a very limited suffrage and called attention to the government of contemporary France, which was virtually a pure autocracy, yet had universal manhood suffrage.[37] *The Nation's* liberalism called for quality, not quantity, in the electorate, and its democratic theory was not to be compressed into the formalism of universal suffrage.

Nevertheless, *The Nation* was an early, if lukewarm, advocate of Negro suffrage, for it felt that the ballot would assist the Negro in defending himself from his late masters.[38] Furthermore, the extension of the suffrage would be a powerful stimulus to the continued elevation of the Negro.[39] But what Godkin asked was "not that the blacks shall be excluded *as blacks*, but that they shall not be admitted to the franchise simply because they are blacks and have been badly treated."[40] *The Nation* endorsed a wide suffrage provided one met certain minimum qualifications such as age, residence, sanity, a "means of support independent of the charity of the State, unstained with crime, and able to read. . . ."[41]

Since no man held a natural right to vote, since universal suffrage was not a requirement of a democracy, it was not only just but imperative that the state extend the franchise only to those who would exercise it intelligently. Thus, the soundest qualification for the suffrage would be an educational one.[42] Throughout this period *The Nation* continued

---

[35] Rollo Ogden, *Life and Letters of Edwin Lawrence Godkin* (New York: The Macmillan Company, 1907), II, 45-46.
[36] *The Nation*, I (1865), 101.
[37] *Ibid.*, p. 134.
[38] *Ibid.*, III (1866), 498.
[39] *Ibid.*, IV (1867), 395.
[40] Ogden, *op. cit.*, II, 46.
[41] *The Nation*, III (1866), 371.
[42] *Ibid.*, p. 498.

to urge the education of the Negro, for the ballot without the prerequisite of an education, would be detrimental not only to the individual but to the state as well.

After 1868, when the Radicals appeared to have complete control over reconstruction, *The Nation* found itself less and less in sympathy with their program. For no longer was the Negro question being dealt with in accordance with the tenets of liberal democracy, but rather was it an instrument that played into the hands of the corrupt politicians. *The Nation* was among the first Northern journals to condemn the carpet-bag regime. Its disillusionment increased as it observed that the Radicals would bestow the franchise on the Negro without first requiring of him minimum educational qualifications. Far better, *The Nation* now admonished its readers, that the Negro be taught "the lesson of self-reliance and self-deliverance" and given fewer "gaseous lectures about his political rights." The ballot alone could be of no use to the Negro as long as he was not considered a "respectable" member of the community. Equality could not be achieved by law, and the whites could not be forced into respecting the Negro. The Negro would never achieve political equality "by merely being able to produce a copy of the . . . Fifteenth Amendment."

The achievement of economic independence *The Nation* felt, would lead to social and political acceptability. Work, earn, and save, it advised the Negro. "Every deposit in a savings-bank is worth ten votes."[43] Doubtless, many Negroes found the practice more difficult than the formula. Nevertheless, *The Nation* saw clearly what the majority of the humanitarian reformers had failed to consider: that equality springs from something far beneath the formal stratum of law. While *The Nation* endorsed the Fifteenth Amendment, it felt that after this, the future for the Negro lay in his own hands.

Whereas some four decades later Carl Schurz could reaffirm his early position on Negro suffrage,[44] *The Nation* soon began to doubt the wisdom of the franchise. Along with Norton and Lowell, it became more concerned with means of improving the quality of the electorate and thus avoiding mediocrity in office rather than ensuring the Negro his vote. Even before reconstruction had ended, *The Nation*, in a caustic editorial on the extension of the suffrage that had followed the war, remarked that the great expectations which the advocates of Negro suffrage had envisioned had proven by "bitter experience" to be a grand illusion.[45] For, shortly after the war

there was, and not unnaturally, an outburst of superstitious reverence for the ballot *per se*. It became in the eyes of vast numbers of people a kind

[43] *Ibid.*, VIII (1869), 125.
[44] Carl Schurz, *The Reminiscences of Carl Schurz* (New York: The McClure Company, 1908), III, 245.
[45] *The Nation*, XVIII (1874), 312.

of fetish or amulet which would give its possessor a wisdom and foresight which had no relation whatever to his character or education; and we led ourselves into the belief that it would work in a year or two a transformation among the ignorant blacks of the South such as neither religion nor philosophy, art nor science, had ever been able to effect among any race of men in centuries.[46]

Still later, when it became apparent that the Southern states would keep Negroes away from the polls, *The Nation* went to the defense of the South against its Northern critics. It pointed out that the disfranchisement of the Negro in the South was largely a question of whether political power was to reside in the hands of that group

which possesses nearly all the property and most of the intelligence and political sense of the community, or shall pass into the hands of a class without property, without education, and without a single political habit or tradition.[47]

The Nation's formula for reconstruction had called for educating the Negro and protecting him in his civil rights. When qualified to meet the educational requirements of an intelligent electorate, he might, like any other citizen facing these same qualifications, possess the franchise. However, its demand for the instruction of the Negro did not extend to the approval of the proposed National Bureau of Education. Such a national agency it felt would challenge "local self-government and respect for individual rights in the delicate matter of the education of their children." Furthermore, it feared this post-war tendency toward "bureau making" in Washington to solve national problems. "It should never be forgotten," it declared, "that all real growth and progress in agriculture, commerce, manufactures, science, or education is from the people, never from the Government. The Government may hinder, but cannot help; a bureau may record progress, but never originate or cause it." "To Govern Well," *The Nation* counselled, "Govern Little."[48] When Senator Blair proposed a bill to give federal aid for education in the South *The Nation* attacked it as "A bill to promote mendicancy.' For it felt that education was a state, not national, concern and that the "worst thing" which could happen "would be an assumption by the nation of a burden which the South has shown herself able to carry alone, and will be all the stronger in the end for having carried alone."[49]

The Nation also opposed federal regulation of elections as a dangerous measure likely to be used for partisan purposes. It preferred to have the local community solve its own racial problems and disparaged the effectiveness of outside interference. "Unfair elections at the South,"

[46] *Ibid.*
[47] *Ibid.*, XXXI (1880), 126.
[48] *Ibid.*, II (1866), 745-746.
[49] *Ibid.*, XXXXII (1886), 142-143.

it observed in 1889, "will cease when public sentiment in the South condemns them—not before."⁵⁰

Within the space of two decades *The Nation* had virtually reversed its approach to the Negro question. Shortly after the war in an article significantly entitled "The One Humanity," it had declared, "The degradation of one part is the degradation of all, and hence the thought we would labor to impress, that every man has both a selfish and a fraternal interest in the elevation of every other man."⁵¹ Now, some twenty-one years later, although it recognized that the Negro "still suffers keenly from injustice," it felt that "the nation no longer has a negro problem to settle."⁵²

Disillusioned over the failure of the Republicans to adopt a reasonable reconstruction program, dismayed that its great expectations of democracy had not been achieved, and discouraged over the rise of "boss" politicians and demagogues who capitalized on the ignorance of their voting constituencies, *The Nation* lost its early hopes for the settlement of the Negro question in accordance with its democratic ideals. Its early enthusiasm for suffrage extension waned rapidly as it saw the privilege abused by illiterate foreigners in the North and ignorant whites and blacks in the South. It now feared for the educated minority in the face of a tyrannous, uneducated majority. For, until now, the term *majority of the people* had generally meant "property-owners, taxpayers, and people of considerable intelligence and business experience,"⁵³ but with the wide extension of the franchise this group was no longer certain of control. *The Nation* associated the influx of uneducated voters with Tweed and Fernando Wood in New York, that "sink of corruption," with Greenbackism and labor legislation, with tariffs, subsidies, and the silver craze; in short, the new majority was the abettor of pollution in politics and heresy in economics. The problem of postwar America, as *The Nation* saw it, was no longer to guarantee the Negro his rights but rather to hold the ground of morality and orthodoxy against the increasing assaults by "the people." "What we are witnessing here," *The Nation* wrote in 1877 of the plan to remonitize silver,

is but the natural result of the doctrine which has been covertly permeating politics now for half a century . . . that men in a mass, or "the people," as it is called are not necessarily moral, and need consult no law but their own will; that . . . as Ben Butler tersely put it, a nation has no conscience.⁵⁴

Thus, when *The Nation* wrote, in 1886, that the United States "no longer has a negro problem to settle," it was not because it was so greatly impressed with the progress of democracy in the past twenty-one

⁵⁰ *Ibid.*, XXXXIX (1889), 403; cf. LXXVII (1903), 182.
⁵¹ *Ibid.*, I (1865), 521.
⁵² *Ibid.*, XXXXIII (1886), 26.
⁵³ *Ibid.*, XXIV (1877), 245.
⁵⁴ *Ibid.*, XXV (1877), 390.

years, but rather because its attention had become so fixed on other "dark shades" in our system. Unionization under the Knights of Labor, "an unwelcome revelation of the lack of intelligence among the masses of the newcomers from abroad," control of legislatures by powerful corporations, "the demoralizing effect of their methods upon public men, are plain to the most careless observer," and the growing admiration for wealth alone as an idol of young men were but a few of the disturbing signs of the times.[55] Nineteenth-century liberalism appeared to be challenged from every quarter and *The Nation* rose to its defence.

The Nation's concept of democracy was posited on an intelligent, educated citizenry. Its liberalism assumed a government of incorruptible, rational men who would rule in accordance with the principles of laissez-faire. The greatest good of the greatest number was not a mandate to violate the sacred laws of trade. *The Nation's* liberal democratic thought made no more room for Ben Butler or Boss Tweed than its political economy did for Henry George or "Pig Iron" Kelley. Faced with a restless majority that pressed for new privileges in post-war America, *The Nation* looked not to the extending of the base of democracy but rather to the raising of it. It was not until the progressive era of a later day that *The Nation* once again took up the cause of the Negro in our democracy and found that "Wrapped up in the caste spirit which would shut the negro out from his political rights is the intention to deny him his human rights." To tell Negroes "to give up their 'nonsense' about political rights and to turn to 'useful pursuits' really meant that what is wanted is a subject class of willing or forced workers."[56]

[55] *Ibid.*, XXXXIII (1886), 26.
[56] *Ibid.*, LXXVII (1903), 182.

CHAPTER II

LIBERAL POLITICAL ECONOMY

"The old nations of the earth," wrote Andrew Carnegie in the year of the Haymarket riot and the collapse of the Knights of Labor, "creep on at a snail's pace; the Republic thunders past with the rush of the express." "Triumphant democracy," Carnegie called it. "In population, in wealth, in annual savings, and in public credit; in freedom from debt, in agriculture, and in manufactures, America already leads the civilized world."[1] To the gentle criticism of George William Curtis that Carnegie had omitted any shadows in his glowing account, the author replied, "My dear friend, *Triumphant Democracy* was written at high noon, when the blazing sun right overhead casts no shadows."[2] Yet the high noon of our industrial development was not without its critics, for from farm and factory came voices of protest. At that time, however, the protest groups were in transition, deserting old banners for new. Greenbackism, by-product of the Granger movement, had fought, spent itself and wasted away. Populism was yet to be born of the Farmers' Alliance. Labor, self-conscious, realistic, and vocal in post-war America, had organized and lost with Powderly's Knights and now was re-forming within Gompers' new American Federation of Labor. It was a time between times for farmer and worker.

Still in the background, many vital industries were growing up, from little corporations to big corporations, and from big corporations into trusts. Within a year the federal government would be given authority to regulate the railroads. In a decade William Jennings Bryan would lead the march against big business. Protesting forces were gathering for battles; the test of democratic liberalism now lay in its responsiveness to those dislocated by our economic system. In this period the battle was drawn over the proper sphere of government activity. Lurking behind the immediate political issues of tariffs and subsidies, greenbacks and silver purchase, railroad regulation and labor legislation, was a basic problem in political economy. Is it the proper function of the government to intervene in the economic arena beyond protecting property and enforcing contracts? Here was the perplexing question which had run the course of American thought; this was the issue which would separate nineteenth-century liberalism from twentieth-century progressivism.

To those who drew upon the writings of Smith, Ricardo, and Mill, *laissez faire* was economic liberalism, and it was the only proper gov-

[1] Andrew Carnegie, *Triumphant Democracy* (New York: Charles Scribner's Sons, 1886), p. 1.
[2] *Ibid.* (Revised Edition, 1893), p. v.

ernmental policy. Such had been the view of Jeffersonian Democrats in their attacks upon the Federalist policy of modified mercantilism. In the age of Jackson this economic liberalism had been heralded as the only proper theory of political economy by such an assorted group as William Cullen Bryant, Francis Lieber, David Dudley Field, Theodore Sedgwick, Jr., and William Leggett.[3] It had fitted the needs of both the agrarian democracy of Jefferson and the more proletarian democracy of Jackson, for it appeared to provide the closest approximation to the beneficent laws of nature in a harmonious universe. "The more I hear on this subject, and the better I understand it," a student retorted to her tutor in an early American economics text, "the greater is my admiration of that wise and beneficent arrangement which has so closely interwoven the interests of all classes of men!"[4]

Some, however, refused to follow the deductive system of the classical school, and turning directly to the American economy, favored the interventionist theory of government. Such a one was Daniel Raymond. "A government," he wrote,

should be like a good shepherd, who supports and nourishes the weak and feeble ones in his flock, until they gain sufficient strength to take their chance with the strong, and does not suffer them to be trampled on, and crushed to the earth by the powerful.[5]

George Bancroft attacked classical political economy, for, he declared, "its abandonment of labor to the unmitigated effects of personal competition can never be accepted as the rule for the dealings of man with man." He predicted that "the masses themselves will gain the knowledge of their rights, courage to assert them, and self-respect to take nothing less." And, with characteristic optimism, he heralded the future "when the heartless jargon of over-production in the midst of want will end in a better science of distribution...."[6]

In spite of our history of tariffs and subsidies, the English classical school became entrenched in our colleges and universities, and no better spokesman for its cause could be found in post-Civil War America than *The Nation* magazine. When the impact of an accelerated industrial revolution was fully felt, *laissez faire* met a more fearful challenge than had been formerly presented by the business advocates of subsidies and tariffs. Labor and farmer groups, together with humanitarian reformers, now put away Adam Smith to demand government interference on their behalf. As these newly organized groups pressed for political

---

[3] Arthur M. Schlesinger, Jr., *The Age of Jackson* (Boston: Little, Brown and Company, 1945), pp. 314-315.
[4] Mrs. Jane H. Marcet, *Conversations on Political Economy* (Philadelphia: Moses Thomas, 1817), p. 365. The author also wrote *Conversations on Chymistry*.
[5] Daniel Raymond, *The Elements of Political Economy* (Baltimore: F. Lucas and E. J. Coale, 1823), II, 13.
[6] George Bancroft, *Miscellanies* (New York: Harper and Brothers, 1855), p. 514.

power, the *Wealth of Nations* changed hands and became the instrument of the conservative forces. From pulpit, press, and public platform the argument over the sphere of government functions was heard. In opposition to the demand for social legislation, *The Nation* chanted the Manchester liberals' old refrain. "Political economy," it declared

has demonstrated that human legislation has its sphere, in attempting to transcend which, no matter how worthy the motive may be, it only works the more injury as it strives to attain an ideal good.[7]

Nature herself had determined the proper relations between labor, capital and agriculture, and these relationships could not be altered without causing the most dire consequences. "The market price," *The Nation* pointed out, ". . . is the necessary price." Labor, too, must stand its chances in the competitive market. "Like all other commodities, it is governed by the natural law of supply and demand."[8] To the Manchester liberal, private property, contracts, hard money, and wealth were all jewels in a delicately balanced economic mechanism—necessary, dependable, and not to be tampered with. Competition was the regulator, keeping the working parts at peak efficiency. This, of course, implied full liberty in a free society. Free man, competing in a free society, determined his own future.

"Economics was regarded as a finished product," R. T. Ely has noted in his autobiography. "One could become an economist by reading a single volume." Being basically a logical system, it required of the student only an understanding of certain primary principles; the rest was simply a matter of deducing from the omnipotent, immutable laws.

It was held that natural laws established certain fundamental principles for all times and places. It was only necessary that we should study these natural laws and follow them to attain the highest state of economic felicity possible to mankind.[9]

From the colleges came the standard exposition of the *laissez faire* system which *The Nation* so heartily supported. Francis Wayland's restatement of classical economics in *The Elements of Political Economy* was the most widely used text in this period.[10] At Columbia, students used Fawcett's *Political Economy for Beginners*.[11] At Harvard, the Alford Professor of Natural Religion, Moral Philosophy, and Civil Polity, observed in his text that the principles of political economy "manifest the contrivance, the wisdom and beneficence of the Deity,

---

[7] *The Nation*, IV (1867), 394.
[8] *Ibid.*, I (1865), 517.
[9] Richart T. Ely, *Ground Under Our Feet* (New York: The Macmillan Company, 1938), pp. 125, 126.
[10] Richard Hofstadter, *Social Darwinism in American Thought* (Philadelphia: University of Pennsylvania Press, 1945), p. 123.
[11] Ely, *loc. cit.*

just as clearly as do the marvellous arrangements of the material universe. . . ."[12] In this harmonious universe, "We are all servants of one another without wishing it, and even without knowing it. . . ."[13] From a former lecturer on public economy at Amherst College, F. Amasa Walker, came *The Science of Wealth,* hailed by *The Nation* as one of the best works in the field. "Fortunately," Walker noted in his preface only months before the panic of '73, "the principles of this science are easily understood, when properly presented. . . ."[14] Here was the proper reply to the Granger movement:

Political economy is a science whose laws may be disturbed in their operation, or made perplexing to observation, by the legislation of the state. Practically, this is the great disturbing force which political economy has encountered in all the past. Wealth is the constant subject of legislation often in direct antagonism to its own laws.[15]

As the popular clamor swelled behind the interventionist theory during the seventies and the eighties, an old champion of the classical school was moved to write a new economics text. Professor A. L. Perry of Williams College, author of numerous college economics books, justified this latest contribution on the grounds that

in recent years the legislation of my country in the matter of cheap money and of artificial restrictions on Trade has run so directly counter to sound Economics in their very core, that I felt it a debt due to my countrymen . . . to help them see and act for themselves in the way of escape from false counsels and impoverishing statutes.[16]

From Yale, William Graham Sumner, fearful that "democracy will be construed as a system of favoring a new privileged class of the many and the poor," advised that free trade would be a greater boon to the poor "than all the devices of all the friends of humanity if they could be realized."[17] It was not intervention that society needed, but rather *laissez faire.* "Let us translate it into blunt English, and it will read, Mind your own business. It is nothing but the doctrine of liberty. Let every man be happy in his own way."[18]

With the colleges of the country thus fortified in the classical theory, little wonder it was that *The Nation* sought to encourage soundly educated men to enter politics. Even before the end of the Civil War,

---

[12] Francis Bowen, *American Political Economy* (New York: Charles Scribner's Sons, 1870), p. 21.
[13] *Ibid.,* p. 22.
[14] Amasa Walker, *The Science of Wealth* (Philadelphia: J. B. Lippincott & Co., 1872), p. vi.
[15] *Ibid.,* p. 20.
[16] Arthur Latham Perry, *Principles of Political Economy* (New York: Charles Scribner's Sons, 1891), p. xi.
[17] William Graham Sumner, *What Social Classes Owe to Each Other* (New York: Harper & Brothers, 1883), pp. 37, 161.
[18] *Ibid.,* p. 120.

Godkin had written to C. E. Norton lamenting that, "The intellect and education of this country have for three generations run into law, divinity, or commerce. Ought we not to try and do something to turn the tide into politics?"[19] With the founding of *The Nation*, Godkin directed his energies toward the goal of a government by educated statesmen, grounded in political economy, rather than the democracy of ill-trained politicians. *The Nation* believed that, if the people were taught the laws of political economy, they would see "how totally independent they are of political feeling, and how ridiculous it is to mix them up with purely moral or political considerations."[20] Economics, politics, and morality were separate spheres, yet when properly coordinated, constituted a sacred trinity. "Any boy of good education," *The Nation* observed,

who chooses to go into a mill or workshop, and make himself master of any branch of industry, and determine to live by it, and stick to it and make a profession of *thoroughness* and *fidelity*, may feel as sure of fortune and influence as it is ever permitted to mortals to feel.[21]

For by the laws of economics as well as those of morality, "the weak, the ignorant, the idle, the shuffers, and the stupid go to the wall . . . the strong and educated, and industrious, and thrifty, and intelligent get most of the good things of this life. . . ."[22]

The Nation was among the first American publications to receive favorably Spencer's interpretation of social evolution.[23] Writing in the same year that Carnegie's *Triumphant Democracy* was published, *The Nation* observed that "The law of the survival of the fittest, although its operation requires to be modified by human charity, is the law under which the human race must exist." Having engrafted Spencerism upon Manchester liberalism, it could now attack intervention in the economic sphere on the grounds that "to attempt by social or political devices to do away with the punishment that falls upon moral weakness, is to engage in a mischievous struggle against a beneficent law of Providence."[24]

The Nation happily accepted the late nineteenth-century synthesis of classical economics, Spencerian science, and Protestant theology. Thus fortified in expressing its disapproval of legislation that would bring positive relief to any group in the economic struggle for existence, its voice was that of conservative America. Its liberalism was that of a previous age, and it spoke now for the *status quo*. Lowell summed up the position of this segment of American thought when he declared in a Boston speech:

[19] Ogden, *op. cit.*, II, 47.
[20] *The Nation*, IX (1869), 66.
[21] *Ibid.*, VII (1868), 524.
[22] *Ibid.*, XV (1872), 293.
[23] Hofstadter, *op. cit.*, pp. 10 ff.
[24] *The Nation*, XXXXIII (1886), 538.

If our politicians would devote to the study and teaching of political economy half the time they spend in trying to agree so as not to agree with the latest attempt of the Knights of Labor to unhorse the Nature of Things, they would be far less harmful to themselves and to the country.[25]

It was the very "Nature of Things" that was at issue.

There were many, however, who did not subscribe to the classical injunction to keep government out of business. To a large extent these writers were intellectual descendants of Alexander Hamilton and Henry Clay and represented what they claimed to be an indigenous American theory, as opposed to the English school. When they looked abroad for arguments at all, they turned generally to the German writers and followers of Frederick List. For the most part, this group was associated with the protectionist policy and sought to maintain an independent, diversified economy through the instrument of a high tariff. But their arguments for protection could hardly stop with business alone, and thus their theories had an influence upon a wide and assorted breed of disciples.

If the classical economists had captured the colleges, so had the interventionists control of Congress and many state legislatures. It was natural then for *The Nation* to feel that the legislative branch of government needed to be "hedged in and fenced about with every sort of restraint and prohibition that can be devised,"[26] for Congressmen, rather than being representatives of the people, now acted as delegates of the people, and as such were subject to the follies and caprices of the rule of mere numbers. What was needed, *The Nation* pointed out, were members "who should sit for the thinking part of the country, who should have a constituency of mind and principle more truly than of numbers."[27]

The Honorable William D. ("Pig Iron") Kelley of Pennsylvania disparaged the efforts of the leading colleges to inculcate their pupils with the *laissez faire* doctrine. It was fortunate, he held, that "the intimate relations of many of the students with the industries and people of the country render the scholasticism of their teachers harmless. . . ."[28] A strong supporter of the high tariff, Kelley nevertheless declared in Congress that "Farmers, Mechanics, and Laborers Need Protection—Capital Can Take Care of Itself."[29] In a volume of his speeches and letters, inscribed to Henry C. Carey, Kelley opened with an assault upon the Manchester school. "The theory that labor . . . is merely a

[25] James Russell Lowell, *Works* (Boston: Houghton, Mifflin and Company, 1894), VI, 183-184.
[26] *The Nation*, XX (1875), 342.
[27] *Ibid.*, III (1866), 272.
[28] William D. Kelley, *Speeches, Addresses and Letters* (Philadelphia: Henry Carey Baird, 1872), p. xx.
[29] *Ibid.*, p. 322.

raw material, and that that nation which pays least for it is wisest and best governed, is inadmissable in a democracy. . . ."[30]

Horace Greeley, in a collection of his essays, dedicated to Henry Clay, observed that the construction of the Erie Canal and its subsequent prosperous effect upon farmer and merchant alike was a tribute to the perspicacity of those who "had not studied political economy in the school of negation and obstruction."[31] The classical contention that individual selfishness results in social gains, Greeley said, "ignores the most vital distinctions, and makes him who amasses most wealth the most useful citizen, contrary to every man's experience and moral perceptions. . . ." "I insist," Greeley added, "that the value to the community of a man's efforts is not indicated or measured by the amount of his resulting gains."[32] And finally, Greeley observed of this dictum of self-interest, "Unhappily, our courts, sheriffs, police, prisons, gibbets, are standing proofs that this can not be relied on."[33] In defiance of the classical school, Greeley defended the labor movement and argued that trade unionism had actually improved, and justifiably so, the condition of the worker. "But all this," he noted, "is 'smoke to the eyes and vinegar to the nose' of the Free-Traders, whose fundamental principle it impugns, whose entire philosophy it conflicts with."[34] Needless to say, *The Nation's* opinion of Greeley was no higher than its opinion of Kelley, whom it despised.

Perhaps the most consistently attacked critic of the classical school, shortly after the war, was Henry C. Carey. For he committed a double sin: not only was he a protectionist, but he utilized a modicum of scholarship to justify his arguments. One of his admirers wrote shortly after his death that, "Dr. Carey was by far the most vigorous and sustained, learned and equipped, versatile and philosophic assailant of the *laissez faire* theory."[35] Even in attacking Carey, *The Nation* would admit he was a man of reputation, which was more than it would grant most of the interventionists. However, in reply to Carey's demand for a high protective tariff, *The Nation* would bring forth the principles of Manchester liberalism.

It is a well-established doctrine of the old political economy . . . that each individual, in either buying from or selling to foreigners, does what is best for his own interest, which he understands better than anybody else; and that what is best for his interest is best for that of the country; that what is true of one person is true of ten thousand. . . .[36]

---

[30] *Ibid.*
[31] Horace Greeley, *Political Economy* (Boston: James R. Osgood and Company, 1871), p. 127.
[32] *Ibid.*, pp. 128-129.
[33] *Ibid.*, pp. 130-131.
[34] *Ibid.*, p. 345.
[35] Van Buren Denslow, *Principles of the Economic Philosophy* (New York: Cassell & Company, Ltd., 1888), p. 16.
[36] *The Nation*, XV (1872), 376.

Carey, like Greeley and Kelley, was a severe critic of English trade practices and felt that the application of them in the United States would impoverish us to the gain of the London merchants.[37] This antipathy toward Britain and British trade practices was as characteristic of this group of writers as was the fondness and respect for ideas and things English a conspicuous feature in the *laissez faire* school.[38]

In considering the reasons why political economy had not been cultivated in America, *The Nation* listed, among others, the slavery controversy. The question of slavery in the United States had become such a primary issue that the study of political economy had been generally neglected. Now that this issue was settled, *The Nation* pressed for a thorough examination of the operation of the laws of trade. Here, in the United States, it observed in 1867, "the political economist has an opportunity of watching the working of the natural laws such as European society never affords him."[39] Though *The Nation* felt that the slavery controversy had had a distracting effect upon the study of political economy, there were others who believed that it had actually stimulated American thinking, and in terms of the interventionist approach. Such a one was Van Buren Denslow, who wrote that "The result of the American contest of 1861-65 tended far more powerfully than any admission by Mr. Mill to give influence and power to American thought." Up to the time of the war, he pointed out, "The government had practiced *laissez faire* toward slavery. . . ." This policy had failed. Thus, "The century, whose chief business it had been to teach that government must not interfere with industry, found its most stupendous effort to be the conduct of the revolution for insuring the payment of wages to servants."[40]

The battle between the economists over the question of governmental intervention in the economic sphere continued with increasing vigor. In the middle 1880's a new group of historians and economists, recently returned from studies in Germany, applied themselves to American political economy. Such men as H. B. Adams, John Bates Clark, Simon Patten, E. J. James, E. R. A. Seligman, and R. T. Ely, following German thinkers somewhat, turned to humanizing the "dismal science."[41] This

---

[37] England and France were on the decline, he felt, but "in accordance with a great law from the study of which we learn that the richest soils are always last to be brought under cultivation, the great powers of the future must be Germany, Russia, and these United States." Henry C. Carey, *Miscellaneous Works* (Philadelphia: Henry Carey Baird, 1875), "Review of the Decade 1857-1867," p. 39.

[38] One writer, describing the effects of free trade on the British farmer, declared that, "So long as the prowess of the British Army extends British markets adequately to keep British spindles going, the ruin of the farmers can be atoned for by the prosperity of the manufacturers. To perceive this has constituted the distinctive function of the Manchester school." Denslow, *op. cit.*, p. 40.

[39] *The Nation*, V (1867), 255, 256.

[40] Denslow, *op. cit.*, p. 17.

[41] Ely, *op. cit.*, p. 121.

group of economists was to have an influence long felt in America. J. B. Clark crusaded against monopoly so as to restore the freely competitive open market and called upon government assistance in this struggle. On the other hand, Patten looked forward to a co-operative, rather than a competitive society, and taught his pupils the virtues of a planned economy.[42] A fresh approach was brought from Germany into American political economy, and it seemed that, "The long controversy between the economists and human beings has ended in the conversion of the economists."[43] Led by Richard T. Ely, these "rebels" founded the American Economic Association, in 1885, whose Prospectus included such unorthodox statements as the following:

We regard the state as an educational and ethical agency whose positive aid is an indispensable condition of human progress. While we recognize the necessity of individual initiative in industrial life, we hold that the doctrine of *laissez faire* is unsafe in politics and unsound in morals. . . . We believe in a progressive development of economic conditions which must be met by corresponding changes of policy.[44]

The Nation lost no time in attacking what it called "the ethical economists." R. T. Ely recounts that *The Nation,* "which was a citadel of conservatism in all matters affecting property and labor, branded me as a radical and a dangerous man. For years, *The Nation* never lost an opportunity to attack and malign me."[45]

In 1886 Ely wrote an open letter urging the Knights of Labor to endorse civil service reform because government ownership of transportation and communication systems (which he recommended) would require good employees. *The Nation*, in commenting on this, noted of Ely that he was "one of several graduates of German universities who have brought across the ocean that curious admixture of sense and nonsense, commonly but wrongly known among us as German political economy." Furthermore, it added, "He is an ardent believer in popular government, which is all right, and he is a yet more ardent supporter of labor movements, which are about the only enemy popular government seems likely to encounter in our time."[46] When Ely's *The Labor Movement in America* appeared, in 1886, *The Nation's* reviewer declared that Ely showed an "intensity of bias, and a bitterness toward all classes

[42] Among Patten's students was a later "New Dealer," Rexford Guy Tugwell.
[43] Cited in Ely, *op. cit.*, p. 144.
[44] *Ibid.*, p. 136. Present at the founding meeting was the young professor, Woodrow Wilson.
[45] *Ibid.*, p. 219.
[46] *The Nation*, XXXXII (1886), 292. See Godkin's attack on the new school of economists in "The Economic Man," *Problems of Modern Democracy* (New York: Charles Scribner's Sons, 1903), third edition. "In short, the new departure which the new schools are all calling for is a new departure in politics, not in political economy. There is hardly a trace of science in their talk any more than in that of city Missionaries. What they are asking us to do is simply to try a hazardous experiment in popular government." P. 176.

of society except one. . . ." Labor discontent, it noted, "is perennial in human nature, and is bound to continue, no matter what measure we take to cure it. We may, perhaps, draw the equally encouraging conclusion that it will do no more harm in the future than in the past." That *The Nation* was distressed over the invasion of the "ethical school" into the stronghold of the classical theory was unmistakable. "Dr. Ely," it stated, "seems to be seriously out of place in a university chair."[47]

Laissez faire was political economy to most educated people in post-Civil War America. As Francis A. Walker observed, "Here it was not made the test of economic orthodoxy, merely. It was used to decide whether a man were an economist at all."[48] The new school of economics was anathema to the orthodox. "The fine old Bentham principle of *laissez faire*," lamented Arthur Latham Perry, "which most English thinkers for a century past have regarded as established forever in the nature of man and in God's plan of providence and government, is gently tossed by Dr. Ely into the wilds of Australian barbarism."[49] And, *The Nation* sadly noted of the "ethical school," "This is a state of things greatly to be regretted. . . . Nine-tenths of them are today singing 'songs of freedom' with socialists and labor agitators, and filling the bellies of the poor with the east wind."[50]

The Nation had urged its readers to study the laws of trade. However, the framework for such studies was the precepts of the classical school, and divergent views therefrom were hardly welcome.

In as much as the slightly unorthodox political economists aroused the displeasure of *The Nation* it was not to be expected that more radical social reformers such as Henry George and Edward Bellamy would be more favorably received. Actually, George did not deviate radically from the classical theory. He was a free-trader, opposed to tariffs and subsidies. He believed in unregulated competition. However, he challenged the right of any man to claim private property in land, because he felt land had been provided for the use of all, and its rental value was determined by society itself. To return land to society, he proposed a tax on its unearned increment, thereby abolishing other forms of taxation. *"It is not necessary,"* George wrote, *"to confiscate land; it is only necessary to confiscate rent. . . ."*[51] Believing that land rent taxes, the single tax, would be sufficient to meet all the revenue requirements of government, he felt that businessman, worker, and farmer would be better off as unused land was released and the savings from other taxes were put into new production and higher wages. Railroads and telegraphs, he wrote, would be nationalized if necessary.

[47] *Ibid.*, XXXXIII (1886), 293-294.
[48] F. A. Walker, "Recent Progress of Political Economy in the United States," *Publications of the American Economic Association*, IV (1889), 26.
[49] Perry, *op. cit.*, p. 252.
[50] *The Nation*, LVIII (1894), 382.
[51] Henry George, *Progress and Poverty* (New York: The Modern Library Edition), p. 405.

George's genuine concern for the poor led him to attack the orthodox political economists. At the University of California in 1877 he queried,

> While they insist upon freedom for capital, while they justify on the ground of utility the selfish greed that seeks to pile fortune on fortune, and the niggard spirit that steels the heart to the wail of distress, what sign of substantial promise do they hold out to the working man save that he should refrain from rearing children. . . ?[52]

In his *Progress and Poverty* George set aside some four chapters to assail the Malthusian theory. "It furnishes a philosophy," he wrote, "by which Dives as he feasts can shut out the image of Lazarus who faints with hunger at his door. . . . For poverty, want, and starvation are by this theory not chargeable either to individual greed or to social maladjustments; they are the inevitable results of universal laws. . . ."[53] Malthus, however, was the starting place for social Darwinists, and *The Nation* came directly to his defense, using India as proof of the Malthusian principle.

At first, *The Nation* found George harmless enough. "Mr. George is not an agrarian, or a communist, or in any sense a disturber of the peace and good order of society."[54] That was before he ran for Mayor of New York. In that canvass, *The Nation*, alarmed at his popularity, found that "the aim and expectation of Henry George's supporters is by a large vote to undo what has been done for law and order."[55] Now it attacked him for advocating dispossessing landowners without compensation, and for stirring up class hatred. A few years later *The Nation* remarked that private ownership of agricultural land had been introduced "by a process of natural selection," and it asked, "If people suddenly destroy land titles in obedience to the theories of Henry George, why will they not abolish other titles in obedience to the theories of Proudhon?"[56] The man who was not a "disturber of the peace and good order of society" had acquired too large and serious a following for the comfort of conservative critics.

Edward Bellamy escaped the full ire of *The Nation* because, apparently, *The Nation* could not take him seriously. Though Bellamy's program, set forth in *Looking Backward*, called for such radical measures as the complete nationalization of industry, regimentation of labor, and equality of income; and his indictment of capitalism for its wastefulness resulting from competition, mistaken undertakings, and depressions, found many adherents, *The Nation* chose to consider him a novelist. Its reviewer found *Looking Backward* "a glowing prophecy and

---

[52] Henry George, Jr., *The Life of Henry George* (Toronto: The Poole Publishing Company, 1900), p. 277.
[53] Henry George, *op. cit.*, p. 99.
[54] *The Nation*, XXXI (1880), 65.
[55] *Ibid.*, XXXXIII (1886), 264.
[56] *Ibid.*, XXXXVIII (1889), 218, 260.

a gospel of peace," and poked a little fun. "Mr. George might object that the author begs the land question . . . but Mr. George himself would rejoice in a realized ideal of socialism such as this. . . ."[57] Bellamy's hero, Julian West, after visiting the Boston slums, stated in words anticipating Bryan's, "I have been in Golgotha . . . I have seen Humanity hanging on a cross!"[58] By the year 2,000, Bellamy wrote, "The epoch of trusts had ended in the Great Trust."[59] The Golden Age had come when poverty and unemployment and slums were things of the past. However, *The Nation* coldly observed, "He who would ask if this be sound political economy, let him ask if Donatello's ears were really furry."[60] Democracy, *The Nation* later noted in regard to the Nationalist group, Bellamy's disciples, "strives to establish equality of opportunities, not equality of recompense," and it "quite as much as Absolutism or Socialism recognizes the promotion of the public good as the basis of individual rights and the measure of individual duties."[61] Bellamy's battle was primarily against capitalism. *The Nation* chose to argue from the vantage point of democracy.

If *The Nation* was not over distressed about Bellamy-ism, it was genuinely disturbed over the rise of socialism abroad and the problem of keeping "the Socialist devil" out at home. For, it noted, "the Red Spectre offers nothing and asks for all."[62] John Stuart Mill, some years earlier had found much of the St. Simonian criticism of Liberalism valid and over a period of time had abandoned some of his original political economy to adopt a position which he described as "qualified Socialism."[63] In his *Autobiography* he declared that he considered "The social problem of the future . . . to be, how to unite the greatest individual liberty of action with a common ownership in the raw material of the globe, and an equal participation of all in the benefits of combined labor."[64]

The Nation approached socialism with a far less sympathetic attitude.

The rich man is called on to strip himself of his riches; the frugal man of his savings; the able man to treat his ability as an incumbrance; and the whole community, as a community, to give up all it loves and glories in. Smoking is to be allowed at funerals, and the men and women are to mate in the streets. Children are to go to the foundling hospital. Whatever power there is anywhere is to be lodged in the hands of the most stupid and incapable.

[57] *Ibid.*, XXXXVI (1888), 266.
[58] Edward Bellamy, *Looking Backward* (New York: The Modern Library Edition), p. 267.
[59] *Ibid.*, p. 41.
[60] *The Nation*, XXXXVI (1888), 266.
[61] *Ibid.*, XXXXVIII (1889), 478.
[62] *Ibid.*, XXVI (1878), 318.
[63] John Stuart Mill, *Autobiography* (New York: Columbia University Press, 1924), pp. 117, 133-134.
[64] *Ibid.*, pp. 162-163.

The lazy are to lie on their backs and the industrious to get nothing for their industry.[65]

What were the sources of this amazing doctrine? To *The Nation*, many of the seeds lay in the "democratic doctrines" which had been openly preached since the French Revolution. Among these was the belief that the numerical majority were not only omniscient but omnipotent, and therefore capable of undertaking any social experiment, without limit or redress. Also, contentment, which the churches had taught "as a Christian virtue for seventeen hundred years, and particularly contentment with one's station in life and worldly surroundings" was now rejected even by "social and religious conservatives." In its place now, discontent was preached as a virtue; a man should "strive continually for fame and wealth." If one fails, the easiest explanation is "the rottenness of society, and the richness of the field it offers to trickery and greed."

Another factor leading to socialism was the shift in means of production from outdoor labor, which "keeps down mental activity and strengthens the love of routine," to indoor factory work, which "stimulates the passion for speculation" and "seems to give the brain a morbid energy which finds relief in imaginary rearrangements of society." Also, the age of rapid scientific developments tended to encourage undue optimism as to "what science may yet accomplish in the future." This, as a result, "filled the working-class mind with fantastic dreams as to the possibility of machinery displacing manual labor, and enabling the race to multiply *ad libitum* without inconvenience." Couple these notions with the current ideas of the "perfectibility of man," and the uneducated are prepared for socialism or some other plan by which "the world can be peopled by what are called 'ladies and gentlemen'. . . ." However, *The Nation* concluded, the tide of socialism will be stemmed, and in the future the government will be given fewer duties and individuals more. "When a human being begins to conduct himself like a wild animal the plea of unhappiness will not be so readily accepted in his defence."[66]

As the late nineteenth-century guardian of Manchester liberalism in the United States, *The Nation* opposed nearly all the political economic movements of that period. Business groups which sought government aid through tariffs and subsidies experienced a sustained and vigorous attack by *The Nation*. It was the tariff that the laborer could blame for his low wages and high living costs; the tariff was to blame for the farmer's high transportation costs and the high prices paid by consumers. The tariff was at the bottom of government corruption, monopolies and trusts, and the growing intervention theory of government. The Credit Mobilier

[65] *The Nation*, XXVI (1878), 318.
[66] *Ibid*.

scandal was the "natural result of a long course of legislation in which the seeds of corruption were thickly sown. The first assaults on the virtue of Congressmen were undoubtedly made through the tariff. . . ." To *The Nation*, the remedy was quite simple.

> The government must get out of the "protective" business and the "subsidy" business and the "improvement" and the "development" business. It must let trade, and commerce, and manufactures, and steamboats, and railroads, and telegraphs alone. It cannot touch them without breeding corruption.[67]

Orthodox economists found some difficulty in explaining the origin of trust and market monopolies in a free and competitive system. *The Nation* found their origin in tariffs and subsidies. To attack the trusts, therefore, remove the tariffs. "The protective tariff," *The Nation* advised the business lobbyists, "is a socialistic contrivance," for it endorsed the theory of direct government intervention in the economic sphere.[68] Tariff tinkering makes clean politics impossible in a democracy based on universal suffrage. "This system would eventually corrupt a community of angels."[69] If you admit the justice of a protective tariff, and the duty of the government to impose it, "you clear the coast for Karl Marx and Juares and Bebel and Bellamy and the whole crowd of social dreamers and firebrands."[70] The responsibility for Coxey's army and the Populists rested with those who preached protectionism, a protectionism which, in truth, never benefited the wage earners for "the people who rob Peter to pay Paul do not, as a rule, pay Paul at all; they keep the money themselves."[71]

As it became increasingly evident that the Republican Party championed a high protective tariff, while Democrats advocated a moderate tariff policy, *The Nation* threw itself into a crusade for Cleveland. "Protection," it declared in 1892, "like negro slavery, is a principle which can not be allowed to stand still. Once conceded to be right in itself, the one movement, as was the case with the other, is morally bound to be advanced into new fields and carried to its remotest logical extremes."[72] Cleveland stood, along with Washington and Lincoln, as the leader of a great revolution against privilege, "the candidate of the people."[73] His aim, as with Washington and Lincoln, was "the perfection of individual liberty, self-government, and unshackled interchange with all the nations of the earth."[74]

---

[67] *Ibid.*, XVI (1873), 68.
[68] *Ibid.*, XXXXIV (1887), 28.
[69] *Ibid.*, LIII (1891), 5.
[70] *Ibid.*, LVIII (1894), 189. The difference between socialists and protectionists was largely one of method and degree. The socialists thought in terms of the perfectibility of man, while "the protectionists openly acknowledge that 'the State' is composed of men who like money and are capable of being corrupted in a good cause."
[71] *Ibid.*, p. 322; XXXXVI (1888), 420.
[72] *Ibid.*, LIV (1892), 478.
[73] *Ibid.*, p. 480.
[74] *Ibid.*, LV (1892), 366.

Cleveland and the liberals won, but theirs was only a temporary victory in the long battle for tariff reform. The history of this period is replete with tariff tinkering, nearly all upwards. It was with considerable regret, and some bitterness, that *The Nation* summed up the history of the Republican Party some years later upon the occasion of the retirement of Aldrich from the Senate. "From 'the party of moral ideas,' from the party of union and freedom and equal rights, it was turned into the party of wealth, of extortion, of intrenched and insolent commercial privilege."[75] With the passing of Cleveland from the political scene, *The Nation* was left with neither party nor candidate.

Writing in 1886 on the occasion of the coming of age of the republic since the end of the Civil War, *The Nation* noted that, though many serious problems had been put behind, still others lay ahead. Of no little consideration for the future was the growing power of corporate wealth which brought undue influence upon the government in order to seek special favors or forestall undesirable legislation.[76] This was the period which saw the sole proprietor, with his unlimited liability, increasingly give way to a collection of proprietors, stockholders, with limited liability. It was the period which first saw the truly revolutionary effects that might be achieved by the collective ownership of the means of production and exchange now made possible by the wide-scale application of the corporate device. Over an expanding, vital area of our economic life the pioneer individual was supplanted by the corporate "person." That the increasing use of the corporation as a form of business organization was putting a strain upon an economic system based on individual enterprise did not appear to *The Nation* to be an ominous development. But the irresponsible use of stockholders' money to purchase privileges from state legislatures did. Thus, while the rise of the modern corporation was a phenomenon capable of assimilation into classical economics, its illegitimate political activities came in for the severest attack. No better illustration of this may be found than in *The Nation's* early attitude toward the railroads. "The locomotive," it observed, "is coming in contact with the framework of our institutions,"[77] and state governments were being brought under its control.

What power commands at Trenton? Is it not the Camden and Amboy? What at Harrisburg? Is it not the Pennsylvania Central? What at Albany? Is it not the New York Central?[78]

While *The Nation* early attacked the railroads and their managers, "soulless corporations" run by "feudal barons," it was because the railroads failed to use adequate safety devices, and the accident rate was high. On the grounds, mainly, of accident prevention, it sought federal regulation of the railroads.

[75] *Ibid.*, XC (1910), 394.
[77] *Ibid.*, XVI (1873), 250.
[76] *Ibid.*, XXXXIII (1886), 26.
[78] *Ibid.*, I (1865), 425.

However, as the farm protest against the railroads became more audible, coherent, and effective, *The Nation*, always an opponent of state regulation, found itself on the side of the railroads.

> When the Grangers had once proclaimed that their object was to "fix rates," or, in other words, to declare by law what proportion of the market value of services they themselves should pay, and that they would not be bound by the terms of their contracts, it was perfectly clear that the Granger movement was rank communism. . . .[79]

The whole scheme of establishing by fiat the rates at which railroads might operate was "spoilation pure and simple—spoilation as flagrant as any ever proposed by Karl Marx or Ben Butler."[80] *The Nation* now found the railroad managers no longer feudal barons; railroad management had come, it said, "by a sort of process of natural selection, to be committed to the hands of what is perhaps the ablest body of men in the United States."[81]

In opposing the Reagan Interstate Commerce bill in 1884, *The Nation* observed that "competition has accomplished most of the ends which Grangerism aimed to secure," therefore, the bill was "superfluous."[82] The best thing Congress could do in the railroad matter was to "keep hands off altogether, or at most confine itself to the systematic collection and publication of statistics."[83] When the bill came up for passage *The Nation* opposed the pooling prohibition and the long and short haul clause. Pooling, it felt, would not become oppressive, nor would any railroad abuse "become really serious in the face of a public opinion which supports so stringent a measure as the one now pending."[84] It expected no beneficial results from the Interstate Commerce Act, "a piece of State socialism at variance with the real interests of the people. . . ."[85]

However, as the Courts moved in to determine reasonable rates under the Act, *The Nation* took a more favorable view of railroad regulation. Justice Brewer's conservative approach was *The Nation's* ideal, for by 1892 *The Nation* was proclaiming, "The railroads need protection more than the general public." Reasonableness was the criterion of rate fixing and the true determination of violations under the Anti-Trust Act and in both instances the ultimate decision should rest with the courts.

In reviewing the history of railroad regulation some ten years after the Interstate Commerce Act was passed, *The Nation* found that the attempt at regulation had failed and properly so.

> The attempt to regulate the interstate business of railways has broken down . . . because it is opposed to the supreme law of this country, which,

[79] *Ibid.*, XXII (1876), 58.
[80] *Ibid.*, XVII (1873), 36.
[81] *Ibid.*, XVI (1873), 249.
[82] *Ibid.*, XXXIX (1884), 540.
[83] *Ibid.*, XXXX (1885), 438.
[84] *Ibid.*, XXXXIII (1886), 517.
[85] *Ibid.*, XXXXIV (1887), 93.

by the agency of the courts, guarantees to every man—and to every corporation—the right to manage his own business.[86]

The courts stood guard with *The Nation* over classical political economy.

Though, by fiction, corporations were considered in law and economics as free individuals in a free enterprise system, a combination of these fictitious individuals, trusts, stood outside both law and accepted theory. Therefore, *The Nation* warned investors against squandering their money in them. "Trusts," *The Nation* advised, "are illegal or extra-legal corporations, created for an anti-social purpose, *i.e.*, the establishment of monopolies." But "the law of competition," it cheerfully predicted, "is not to be circumvented," and "nothing can prevent new capital and labor from entering the field."[87] Even the Standard Oil Trust "will be put to death somehow and sometime, most probably by its own vaulting ambition."[88] The only cure for the trust ailment that *The Nation* recommended was the withdrawal of tariff protection. Beyond that, it relied on competition. The Sherman Anti-Trust Act seemed of so little consequence that it passed without editorial comment from *The Nation*. And by 1892 *The Nation* could observe that we did not require "any more stringent legislation, Federal or State, to protect the general public against the extortions of monopolies" beyond removing tariff protection.[89] In fact, "it may be that the evolution of the corporation will in time distinctly favor individualism."[90]

By 1897, *The Nation* was defending trusts on the grounds of reduced costs to the consumer and attacking the "whole scheme of criminal legislation against Trusts and monopolies, federal and state, which has all been enacted wtihin a few years at the demand of agitators. . . ."[91] Congressional regulation of railroads and trusts was simply a part of the current "antiproperty craze."[92] Anticipating future developments, *The Nation* pleaded that if the Sherman Act must remain, it should be interpreted to mean only unreasonable contracts in restraint of trade.[93] In this, it had a strong ally in Justice Brewer, a man "thoroughly imbued with the spirit of the founders of our institutions" who "never hesitated to stem the current of popular opinion whenever he dissented from it."[94] In condoning trusts and accepting the status of supercorporations, *The Nation* endorsed the late nineteenth-century corollary to classical political economy, and its drastic modification of early Manchester liberalism.

Among the problems still before the triumphant democracy of 1886 *The Nation* listed the Knights of Labor and trade-unionism. Having but little sympathy with labor as a class, *The Nation* exhibited only the

[86] *Ibid.*, LXVI (1898), 220.
[88] *Ibid.*, XXXXIV (1887), 381.
[90] *Ibid.*, LXI (1895), 59.
[92] *Ibid.*, LXIV (1897), 257.
[94] *Ibid.*, XC (1910), 305.
[87] *Ibid.*, XXXXV (1887), 68.
[89] *Ibid.*, XIV (1892), 277.
[91] *Ibid.*, LXV (1897), 44.
[93] *Ibid.*, p. 236.

crudest understanding of the labor movement. It feared for the country as it believed that Terence Powderly and his mystic Knights were out to capture America by storm and violence. It relaxed, momentarily, only when the Knights collapsed and the old pattern was restored, the pattern which *The Nation* thought of as the natural order of things. "The civil-service reformers . . . wear their swallow tails and white cravats; and society goes on in the old way, improving solely through toil and industry, the spread of knowledge, the progress of science and invention, and the strenuous exertions of the great mass of men to abolish their own poverty."[95]

That labor would have to combine to compete with combined capital *The Nation* acknowledged. "We have always held," it declared in 1883, "that to talk of the laborer as a free agent in his negotiations with the capitalist, unless he had a labor organization at his back, was a mockery."[96] However, the uses of a trade union were not so clearly defined, while its deficiencies were emphasized. Unions tried to hold their members "down to the level of the most stupid, or slow, or indolent, or contented."[97] They tried to encumber progress by demanding mediocrity, and by curtailing individual initiative and effort. "They seek to overthrow in the moral world the law of the survival of the fittest. . . . They insist that all shall survive, both the fit and the unfit; that virtue shall not have even the reward of achievement, and that the qualities which most distinguish man from the brutes shall not profit any individual man materially."[98] Basically, as *The Nation* saw it, the conflict between labor and capital was simply "a misnomer for the conflict between thrift and idleness."[99] And in *The Nation's* stern Calvinistic world, inevitably there must be "the malingerer, the drunkard, the spendthrift, the rogue, the lazy and idle and vicious thousands who every year, from one cause or another, lose their places on the ladder of life, and drop into the ditch to grovel in hopeless and often angry and venomous poverty."[100]

The labor movement as it developed in post-war America was contrary not only to *The Nation's* economics but to its code of social ethics as well. The reader is left with some uncertainty as to just what purpose trade-unionism might legitimately serve. That it was inevitable, *The Nation* granted, but that unionism might improve wages or decrease hours of work was hardly consistent with orthodox economics. As late as 1888 *The Nation* still clung to the wage-fund theory of payment. "Wages," it declared, "whether high or low are, at any given time, the quotient reached by dividing the wages-fund of that particular time by the number of laborers. . . ."[101] Furthermore, the question was purely an economic one, entirely removed from any concept of social justice.

[95] *Ibid.*, XXXXVII (1888), 307.
[96] *Ibid.*, XXXVII (1883), 428.
[97] *Ibid.*, XXXII (1886), 376.
[98] *Ibid.*, XXXXIII (1886), 305.
[99] *Ibid.*, XXXXIII (1886), 345.
[100] *Ibid.*, XXV (1877), 131.
[101] *Ibid.*, XXXXVII (1888), 165.

There is not even any just claim for the minimum wages necessary to keep a man and his family from starvation. . . . From an employer, a man is not entitled to an atom more than the employer is willing to give in a free market.[102]

With such an approach, *The Nation* could endorse the right to strike, for that was simply a refusal to work under certain conditions, but the corollary of this, the prevention of others from taking up the vacated jobs at those conditions, *The Nation* found barbarous. Any man might quit his job, but no man had the right to interfere wtih strikebreakers, for that would introduce compulsion into the free market. Little wonder that *The Nation* found the difference between "boycotting and bomb-throwing" to be simply "one of degree."[103]

There was no obligation upon an employer, or society in general, to pay a given rate of wages. Society was only obligated to protect "life and property and personal rights to all its members, and nothing more." Even hospitals, almshouses and asylums for the indigent were not obligations of society but rather were agencies designed "not merely to relieve human suffering but to bless the giver equally with the receiver."[104] And yet, *The Nation* lamented that labor had failed to keep up in "culture with the growth of invention" and so failed to provide an adequate market for goods. Opposed to legislative remedies or compulsory union tactics, it thought of labor as it came to think of the Negro problem—something to be solved only by enlightenment. As it said of the manual laborers in 1878,

the great economical as well as moral problem of our time is to raise him as a consumer by rational and healthful process [for] his ambition thus far too often does not go beyond a diminution of his hours of labor.[105]

The Nation's economic liberalism had assimilated, without any great difficulty, corporations and super-corporations into its individualism. They were still pure and simple individual economic bargaining units. Such was not true of labor unions; their component corporeality was evidence enough against them. Therefore it sought to apply the restraint of trade doctrine against them after the passage of the Sherman Act.[106] And when the Pullman Strike came in 1894, *The Nation* likened the issue to the anti-slavery crusade. "The insidious attack of labor-unions on the power of the government, with the boycott and a universal sympathetic strike as weapons, also has its instructive analogies with the assault of slavery upon the national life." Fortunately, however, *The Nation* concluded, the President has the required power "not only to suppress mobs, but to overcome anarchist Governors."[107]

The Nation viewed with no less alarm the demand for governmental assistance to ameliorate the conditions of labor. The eight-hour day

[102] *Ibid.*, XXXX (1885), 91.
[104] *Ibid.*, XXV (1877), 85.
[106] *Ibid.*, LXV (1897), 64.
[103] *Ibid.*, XXXXII (1886), 391.
[105] *Ibid.*, XXVII (1878), 207.
[107] *Ibid.*, LIX (1894), 22, 23.

movement, led by Ira Steward shortly after the war, advocated a theory of government intervention which was contrary to all the established laws of political economy.[108] The argument that if the government could fix ten hours a day, as was true in several of the states, it could also fix eight, *The Nation* found fallacious on the ground that ten hours had been really established by natural economic forces rather than by legislative edict.[109] Nor was ten hours detrimental to labor either from the point of view of health or social standards. For with ten hours employed in work, eight hours for sleep and one and one-half hours for meals, "This leaves four and a half hours for recreation and culture."[110] It feared that the effect of government interference with the conditions of labor would be "to create the belief that the theory that there is such a thing as a market rate of wages is a mere invention of the capitalists; that the proper rate of wages is what will provide a man and his family with 'a comfortable subsistence' and that this rate, be it much or be it little, all employers ought to pay and be made to pay...."[111]

Only with the greatest of misgivings did *The Nation* observe the rise of social legislation abroad. Germany's accident and sickness insurance programs it found "completely alien to our manner of approaching social problems" and tending to destroy the "incentives to prudence" while removing the "preventive checks to population."[112] That England should eventually come to consider broad social legislation was even more distressing.

We cannot but regard it as ominous that this country, which maintained and gave to the world the great principle of resistance to all governmental encroachment upon the liberties of the subject, should be threatened with socialistic oppression.[113]

In *The Nation's* individualistic world of free agents, rational men contracted their services and determined their own futures in accordance with the dictates of self-interest, the only outer limits to their conduct being the natural laws of trade, and, in substance much the same thing, the immutable laws of morality. Thus, individual liberty and governmental authority stood poles apart. That the extension of governmental authority could actually increase the realm of individual liberty was logically impossible to *The Nation*, for all relationships outside of governmental control were of a voluntary nature, freely willed and contracted. Therefore, it rejoiced to see state labor laws discarded by the courts, and when in *Tilt v. Illinois* the State Supreme Court found an eight hour law for women in factories unconstitutional, *The Nation* con-

---

[108] *Ibid.*, I (1865), 517.
[109] *Ibid.*, p. 615.
[110] *Ibid.*, II (1866), 413.
[111] *Ibid.*, XIV (1872), 386.
[112] *Ibid.*, XXXX (1885), 175; XXXXV (1887), 412.
[113] *Ibid.*, LX (1895), 197.

gratulated the court. The court, it declared, stated "boldly and clearly that old English principle which sets the freedom of the citizen above State tutelage, even when the latter presents itself under the new mask of the labor vote, with the old excuse that it is all for his own good."[114]

The Nation approached the labor question in much the same spirit as William Graham Sumner. Sumner, too, looked to a society based on contract, rationalistic, "realistic, cold, and matter-of-fact." In a society which had its basis in contract, there was no place for sentimental coddling. "A society based on contract is a society of free and independent men, who form ties without favor or obligation. . . ."[115] Therefore, Sumner reasoned, in a free society, no man was obligated to help another, and should he do so, his interference would only serve to upset the natural order of things.

If words like wise and foolish, thrifty and extravagant, prudent and negligent, have any meaning in language, then it must make some difference how people behave in this world, and the difference will appear in the position they acquire in the body of society, and in relation to the chances of life.[116]

Holding to the wage-fund theory, Sumner deplored the union tactics of strike and boycott as a means of achieving increased pay. It interfered with the free competition among laborers for jobs, and thereby upset the contractual relationship of independent agents. "The employers of the United States—as a class, proper exceptions being understood—have no advantage over their workmen. . . . The advantage, taking good and bad times together, is with the workmen."[117] Thus Sumner, like *The Nation*, advocated a strict adherence to orthodox political economy. "Here we are, then," he wrote, "once more back at the old doctrine—*Laissez faire*. . . . Let every man be happy in his own way."[118] If Sumner was right, social legislation was wrong.

This was as well the basic approach of *The Nation*. The labor problem of post-war America was to be dealt with only in terms of pre-war dogma. "Do not let us convert it," *The Nation* wrote of America in 1886, "into a republic of kindly patricians charged with the board, lodging, washing, and amusement of a vast and discontented proletariat."[119]

The Nation's disrespect for the labor economists was equalled only by its utter contempt for agrarian politicians. For not only did the Granger and Populist movements express themselves in a demand for railroad and warehouse regulation; they sought to violate the sacredness of the currency and so impair the honorable obligation of contracts.

---

[114] *Ibid.*, p. 251.
[115] William Graham Sumner, *What Social Classes Owe to Each Other* (New York: Harper & Brothers, 1883), pp. 25-27.
[116] *Ibid.*, p. 167.
[117] *Ibid.*, p. 99.
[118] *Ibid.*, p. 120.
[119] *The Nation*, XXXXII (1886), 419.

This, to *The Nation*, was not only a violation of the Constitution and the laws of trade, but of morality itself.

The issue over the currency first presented itself shortly after the war, and *The Nation* entered the controversy at the beginning, pleading for immediate resumption of specie payment. When its Greenback opponents asked for the continued issuance of irredeemable paper money, *The Nation* pointed out that money, to be money, must have intrinsic value. This value cannot be set by the government but is established by the laws of trade. To the classical economist, gold was the only metal that possessed the full requirements of money. Gold, in fact, was the "only money known to the Constitution."[120] When, however, the Greenback issue passed out of the realm of pure economics and into the field of radical politics, *The Nation* fought from the fortress of morality. And when specie payment was finally resumed, *The Nation* wrote of the Greenback period that "the moral mischief it has wrought, though less palpable, is deeper, and more widespread than the financial...."[121]

This moral mischief soon became evident again in the silver agitation. The demand to repeal the so-called "Crime of '73" was basically an attack upon "the very class on whose skill, judgment, and integrity the prosperity of the community depends, and to whose boldness the material progress of the United States has been due."[122] As such, the movement was to *The Nation* simply an attempt to spread "class-hatred." And, later, when the Sherman Silver Purchase Act was passed *The Nation* described it as a "socialistic contrivance of gigantic proportions."[123] Being so bitterly opposed to any theories of money other than the gold standard, *The Nation* had little patience with the agrarian insurgents. When the Wisconsin Alliance movement blossomed into the People's Party, *The Nation* identified it as "a combination of all the worse elements in the community."[124] Coxey's Army was described as a "collection of tramps and criminals."[125]

The American farmer, *The Nation* found, "as ignorant and credulous and suspicious as European peasants" for, "Instead of understanding economical phenomena, they think these are the result of a conspiracy."[126]

When the issue came to a head and Bryan was nominated on a silver platform, *The Nation* sent out the challenge: "If the party of repudiators cannot be put down, the republic cannot be preserved and is not worth preserving."[127] No wonder that the McKinley victory was hailed by *The Nation* as a triumph of civilization over "the still surviving barbarism bred by slavery in the South and the reckless spirit of adventure in the mining-camps of the far West." Of the North Eastern vote for McKinley *The Nation* wrote: "We have all the great dominating

[120] *Ibid.*, VII (1868), 164.
[122] *Ibid.*, XXVI (1878), 163.
[124] *Ibid.*, XXXXIV (1887), 264.
[126] *Ibid.*, LXIII (1896), 323.
[121] *Ibid.*, XXII (1876), 378.
[123] *Ibid.*, L (1890), 502.
[125] *Ibid.*, XVIII (1894), 306.
[127] *Ibid.*, LXIII (1896), 43.

forces of the nation which make for intelligence and righteousness massed in a solid body, in the most impressive vindication of democracy governing according to law and justice that the country has ever seen."[128]

"New occasions teach new duties; Time makes ancient good uncouth," James Russell Lowell had written in 1844 in exhorting his countrymen to join the anti-slavery crusade and strike a telling blow for freedom. From Boston and the surrounding centers of northern culture came an enthusiastic response, swelling through the years until it culminated triumphantly in the winning of the Civil War. With the war over and slavery abolished, Boston intellectual leaders, contrary to Lowell's early injunction, tended to settle down to Back Bay complacency, and Cambridge critics turned their efforts to more scholarly pursuits. When met with the vulgar problems arising out of America's post-war economic expansion, they pinned their hopes on ancient doctrine. "It was sixty years before the leaven of Adam Smith impregnated the whole sluggish lump of British opinion, and we are a batch of the same dough."[129] Thus did Lowell himself "attempt the Future's portal with the Past's blood-rusted key."

Only a few intellectual mavericks continued the struggle for liberty. Wendell Phillips, in adjourning the American Anti-Slavery Society in 1870, called upon his associates to continue the battle. "Welcome new duties!" he said. "We sheathe no sword. We only turn the front of the army upon a new foe."[130] Phillips, with his usual enthusiasm threw himself into the labor movement and ran for Governor of Massachusetts on the Labor Party's ticket.

Addressing the intellectual leaders of America on the occasion of the Centennial Anniversary of the Phi Beta Kappa of Harvard, Phillips observed, "Almost all the great truths relating to society were not the result of scholarly meditation . . . but have been first heard in the solemn protests of martyred patriotism and the loud cries of crushed and starving labor." And to the distinguished audience he concluded with the challenge, "Sit not, like the figure on our silver coin, looking ever backward."[131] For the most part, however, his words went unheeded among the intellectuals.

The Nation, as spokesman for the intellectual liberals of an older day, sought an interpretation of late nineteenth-century economic development in terms of a political economy which had in practice long departed, but whose lingering spirit now served the most conservative interests. In so doing, its battle for static liberalism in an age of dynamic industrialism was a battle for the *status quo*. Human rights succumbed to property rights. Ironically enough, the old liberalism was now placed in battle against the new progressivism.

[128] *Ibid.*, p. 358. [129] Lowell, *op. cit.*, VI, 183.
[130] Carlos Martyn, *Wendell Phillips: The Agitator* (New York: Funk & Wagnalls, 1890), p. 372.
[131] *Ibid.*, p. 391.

CHAPTER III

RESPECTABLE REFORM

"There is a school of pessimists growing up among us," Carl Schurz observed in 1892, "who, whenever anything goes wrong, are ready to declare democratic government a failure and to despair of the Republic."[1] Democracy in America, like democracy elsewhere in the nineteenth century, was no longer an *a priori* blueprint of government, but a system whose virtues as well as deficiencies could be ascertained by observation. The high early expectations of democracy were now matched against its late nineteenth-century results, and the conclusions of the intellectual leaders were unenthusiastic. Gone was the buoyant optimism of 1865; in its place was cautious, at times caustic, criticism. Though only a few would say democracy had proved a failure, most would hold that its virtues in theory had been greatly overestimated, and its deficiencies in practice scarcely anticipated. "I, for my part," said Schurz,

although being beyond the time of youthful illusions, believe that a democratic republic will prove the most excellent form of government, if administered, not necessarily by angels, but by a fairly virtuous, self-respecting, patient, self-restraining, sensible, industrious, liberty-peace- and order-loving people. . . .[2]

Walt Whitman, the poet of democracy, was simply expressing the temper of the times when in *Democratic Vistas*, he said, "It is useless to deny it: Democracy grows rankly up the thickest, noxious, deadliest plants and fruits of all. . . ." And, Whitman asked, "unwieldly and immense, who shall hold in behemoth? who bridle leviathan?"[3]

Democracy now became the scape-goat for nearly all the social ills that beset society—cultural, economic, as well as political. Literary leaders attacked democracy for its impoverished cultural standards and its catering to ignorance. On the centenary of American democracy Lowell wrote nostalgically of the days of John Adams. "I wish I could feel, as I did then," he said, "that we were a chosen people, with a still valid claim to divine interpositions. It is from an opposite quarter that most of our providences seem to come now. . . . Is Democracy doomed by its very nature to a dead level of commonplace?"[4] Charles Eliot Norton

[1] Frederic Bancroft, *op. cit.*, V, 88.
[2] *Loc. cit.*
[3] Walt Whitman, *The Complete Writings of Walt Whitman* (New York: G. P. Putnam's Sons, 1902), II, 143.
[4] Charles Eliot Norton (ed.), *Letters of James Russell Lowell* (New York: Harper & Brothers, 1894), II, 173.

wrote Leslie Stephen that "The rise of the democracy to power in America and in Europe is not, as has been hoped, to be a safeguard of peace and civilization. It is the rise of the uncivilized, whom no school education can suffice to provide with intelligence and reason."[5] And to Lowell, Norton expressed his concern over the "lowering of the moral standard in a democracy like ours to the level of those whose moral sense is in their trowsers (*sic*) and not in their breastpocket."[6] On another occasion Norton wrote, "The rise of Democracy is for the time fatal to social accomplishments and arts."[7]

That so many American men of letters and culture actually felt democracy was afflicted with the diseases of mediocrity and sought some refuge from it, gave point and some pain to Lecky's disparaging comment on the talented Americans who "sought in European life a more congenial atmosphere than they could find at home."[8] Lecky's two-volume criticism of democracy rated an admiring review in *The Nation*.

> Ignorance, so far as it is vested with power, tends to drive out intelligence, just as a debased currency tends to drive out gold. . . . No American of mature years can read Mr. Lecky's book without feeling that the experience of his own country furnishes a great deal of the strongest proof in it.[9]

American democracy, criticized by its adherents and castigated by its opponents, now found itself on the defensive, and *The Nation*, though it did not despair of democracy, spearheaded the domestic criticism.

Basically, the attack on democracy, at home and abroad, was an attack on the social system which it was felt resulted from democracy. The shallow standards, crass materialism, "cheap" millionaires, and secret caucuses of the late nineteenth century were criticized equally by *The Nation*. To the critics Boss Tweed and Jay Gould, Powderly and Vanderbilt, Bryan and Mark Hanna, the shabby and the ornate of the Gilded Age were all by-products of democracy; and, looking ever backward the intellectual elite sought to check the advance of a social system which seemed destined to destroy the values and the standards of an earlier day. Compounding politics, economics, and morality into a static system of absolute values, *The Nation* found in 1865 that "Providence has so arranged it that the rigid observance of the great laws of morality, rigid respect for justice and individual rights on the part of communities, is always the surest road to material wealth."[10]

Against this dictum all political movements of the late nineteenth century were judged, and if found wanting, were condemned on the grounds

---
[5] Charles Eliot Norton, *Letters of Charles Eliot Norton* (Boston: Houghton, Mifflin Company, 1913), II, 236-237.
[6] *Ibid.*, p. 166.
[7] *Ibid.*, p. 235.
[8] William Edward Lecky, *Democracy and Liberty* (New York: Longmans, Green, and Co., 1896), I, 131.
[9] *The Nation*, LXII (1896), 381.
[10] *Ibid.*, I (1865), 581.

of immorality and corruption. *The Nation's* standard of moral purity caused it to think most of the contemporary socio-economic and political movements corrupting influences. Among the sources of corruption were the tariff, special legislation, subsidies, state regulation of railroads, and any government paternalism or interference with business. The issue of Greenbacks as legal tender, the spoils system, like the nominating convention and the party caucus, were most corrupting influences. The silver advocates, like the eight-hour day advocates and the woman's suffrage supporters, played into the hands of corruption. Corruption came inevitably with an elective judiciary holding short terms of office. It also came with the increasing number of ignorant persons in politics and the disappearance of great men from public life. *The Nation* set to work to root out corruption wherever it saw it, and it saw corruption nearly everywhere. Those whose standard of morality reduced the basic difference between a Greenbacker and a Mugwump to one of character could have little sympathy with contemporary politics.

Symptomatic of the ills of democracy was the rise of reform clubs and organizations throughout the North East in the post-Civil War period. Dedicated to the task of purifying politics these organizations held meetings, invited influential speakers, pressed for the extension of the merit system, urged independence in politics, and sought a more active participation of educated men in political affairs. Speaking before the Reform Club of New York in 1888 on the topic, "The Independent in Politics," Lowell urged his fellow citizens to adopt an independent course, free from the shackles of either party, and thereby "emancipate the respectable white man" as they had once emancipated the Negro. He recounted how the Frenchman Guizot had once asked him how long he thought the republic would last. "I replied," said Lowell, " 'So long as the ideas of the men who founded it continue dominant,' " and, added Lowell significantly, "he assented." Now the ideas of the founding fathers were endangered; from every quarter the system seemed to be under attack. "Our leaders no longer lead," Lowell said, "but are as skilful as Indians in following the faintest trail of public opinion. I find it generally admitted that our moral standard in politics has been lowered, and is every day going lower."[11]

What had happened to society that democracy seemed so much at fault? Perhaps the problem had actually been raised some years earlier by de Tocqueville in his observations on Jacksonian democracy. "Can it be believed," he wrote at that time, "that the democracy which has overthrown the feudal system, and vanquished kings, will retreat before tradesmen and capitalists."[12] The radical political economic movements of the 1870's, '80's and '90's all were concerned with a more democratic

[11] Lowell, *op. cit.*, VI, 201, 207, 220.
[12] Alexis de Tocqueville, *American Institutions* (Boston: John Allyn, 1874), I, 5-6.

control over the economic system, and in so seeking to extend democracy, sought in effect, to restrict capitalism. In the conflict between the economic and the political system, *The Nation* tended to defend the former by modifying the latter. Charles Francis Adams, Jr., expressed in a sense *The Nation*'s attitude when he wrote with regret of "the growing tendency to excessive legislation. . . . For myself, I don't believe in it. I never have believed in it; and for this reason, perhaps, have failed to be in sympathy with the sturdy champions of the 'Dear Peepul.'" The man who at one time had headed the Massachusetts Railway Commission, and at another had been president of the Union Pacific had little faith in majority rule when it led to economic heresy. "The lot of the man who talks of Reason, Publicity and Patience," he wrote of his class, "now differs not greatly from the lot of him who three centuries ago questioned Divine Right. . . ."[13] This point was further emphasized by James Bryce when he wrote that "the lamentations with which old-fashioned English thinkers accompany the march of legislation are in America scarcely heard and wholly unheeded."[14]

The failure of modern democracy to accede to the tenets of the old economic liberalism made it vulnerable also to the attacks of some of its unfriendly adversaries. Henry Sumner Maine decried popular government for being opposed to scientific truth. "Universal suffrage which today excludes Free Trade from the United States, would certainly have prohibited the spinning-jenny and the power-loom." The survival of the fittest theory, "the central truth of all biological science," and its economic interpretation, was now opposed by the masses and "thrust into the background by those whom the multitude permits to lead it."[15] Social amelioration seemed a fatal tendency of popular government. A decade later, Lecky noted that "The two things that men in middle age have seen most discredited among their contemporaries are probably free contract and free trade." And as an "apparent accompaniment of modern democracy," Lecky observed "The expansion of the authority and the multiplication of the functions of the State . . . especially in the field of social regulation. . . ."[16] Maine and Lecky, Carlyle and Ruskin, Stephen and Arnold voiced the English conservative attack upon the democratic system. American intellectual leaders, faithful to the old liberalism, still retained faith in democracy, but in point of specific criticism, they were not far distant from their English brethren. Lippincott, in his *Victorian Critics of Democracy*, said: "The protests of the prophets, Carlyle, Ruskin, and Arnold, and of the technical crit-

[13] Charles Francis Adams, Jr., *1835-1915, An Autobiography* (Boston: Houghton, Mifflin Company, 1916), pp. 175-176.
[14] James Bryce, *The American Commonwealth* (London: Macmillan and Co., 1891, 2nd ed.), II, 423.
[15] Sir Henry Sumner Maine, *Popular Government* (London: John Murray, 1885), pp. 36-37.
[16] Lecky, *op. cit.*, I, 257-258.

ics, Stephen, Maine, and Lecky, against democracy was a protest against the rise of the common man."[17] To this protest *The Nation*, in the name of liberalism, added its voice.

The old liberalism had looked upon economic liberty as freedom from governmental control and personal liberty as freedom from chattel slavery. Given these basic liberties, it assumed that rational men, following their own self-interest in a harmonious universe, would elect a government of intelligent men, men whose education taught the wisdom of abiding by the natural laws of political economy. A majority composed of such an electorate was the fit basis for democratic government. The majority, *The Nation* wrote in 1866, "may often decide wrongly, but not oftener than the minority. . . ."[18] During reconstruction *The Nation* said in effect that ultimately it was the majority and not the Supreme Court which must decide the correctness of constitutional interpretations. And to those who were repelled by this notion it added, "The idea that there is something very horrible in being dependent on the majority of a Christian state for liberty and security . . . is the product of that species of fetish worship of which the Constitution has long been the object."[19]

However, with the influx of foreigners into the cities, evidences of carpet-bag rule in the South, and the increasing radicalism of farmer-labor politics, *The Nation* tended to lose faith in the majority and to take refuge behind the courts and the Constitution. No longer was the majority content simply to place and replace men in public office, but it now turned to solving the most delicate social and economic problems. "In these days," *The Nation* wrote in 1868, "if the doors of the future are once thrown open to what are called 'the masses,' and they catch even one glimpse of the splendid possibilities which lie within it, it is in vain to close them again. The vision never leaves their minds."[20]

Majority rule was a tenet of the old liberalism, for it was assumed that self-interest would impose on the majority self-restraint. Self-restraint, however, seemed not to be a characteristic of the new age, and the rise of the ignorant and the poor to political power caused *The Nation*, like so many others, to seek some other checks upon popular control. "We have got so accustomed to having things decided by majorities," *The Nation* wrote of the new trend, "that many people are almost disposed to doubt the discovery of a new planet till the astronomer has submitted his observations to a popular vote. . . ."[21]

The Nation believed that the modern demagogue came out of the demand by the majority of the people for a controlling voice in social

[17] Benjamin Evans Lippincott, *Victorian Critics of Democracy* (Minneapolis: The University of Minnesota Press, 1938), p. 253.
[18] *The Nation*, II (1866), 468.
[19] *Ibid.*, V (1867), 210.
[20] *Ibid.*, VI (1868), 206.
[21] *Ibid.*, IX (1869), 381.

and economic questions. The democratic emphasis on equality tended to destroy or at least weaken the requirements of special fitness for leadership, thus making way for the irresponsible charlatan. For now the "people found themselves wanting not great minds to reason, counsel, and control, but obedient agents to carry out the popular instructions."[22] Reformers such as *The Nation* saw in the Tweed Ring in New York the horrible example of the problems of modern democracy. As a starting place for reform *The Nation* urged "an end of humbug and deception." Now, it said,

"We must openly acknowledge that a very large proportion of our voters [New York] are ignorant and grossly corrupt persons, to whom the rule of a Boss is entirely acceptable, and who are led into setting it up both by their inability to comprehend any other, and by their overpowering anxiety about their daily bread."[23]

Because political power had shifted, so E. L. Godkin thought, from "the rich to the poor," it was to be expected that the legislation and administration of the democracy would reflect this change. To the working classes, "the legislation which excites most attention is apt to be legislation which in some way promises an increase of physical comfort." Godkin, writing on the decline of legislative assemblies, found that increasingly "the work of government is falling into the hands of men to whom even small pay is important, and who are suspected of adding to their income by corruption."[24] Even more distressing to the democracy was the "strong tendency to treat public offices as 'plums' rather than trusts . . . and to consider indifference to the salary as a positive disqualification."[25] With the legislative and executive branches of the government in the hands of the poor and ignorant, the last defense of the older liberalism against the advancing democracy lay in the courts. This branch of government *The Nation* and its followers stoutly defended against any steps toward popular control.

Some indication that all was not well with democracy as America approached the end of the century is given in the fact that the editor of *The Nation* saw fit to publish two books within the space of two years on the subject. *Problems of Modern Democracy* and *Unforseen Tendencies of Democracies* are not eulogistic titles, nor were their contents overly optimistic estimates of the future of democracy. There was still hope, however, if democracy would apply to the present the lessons of experience, root out corruption, and so return to the path of righteousness.

[22] *Ibid.*, XV (1872), 196.
[23] *Ibid.*, XXI (1875), 289.
[24] E. L. Godkin, *Unforeseen Tendencies of Democracy* (Boston: Houghton, Mifflin and Company, 1898), p. 224.
[25] E. L. Godkin, *Problems of Modern Democracy* (New York: Charles Scribner's Sons, 1903), p. 196.

While democracy was threatened by the power of the poor, it also stood in dire danger from the rich. Liberal democracy was basically middle-class in its attitude. If it failed to be duly sympathetic with the poor, nevertheless, the only aristocracy it recognized was that of intellect. Though it accepted Spencerian economics, it rejected the cultural implications of this theory. Social fitness was still determined by character and education. Thus liberalism found itself in the awkward position of defending the economic system which made great acquisitions of wealth possible while decrying the social standards which were its concomitant. The ruthless amoral search for wealth could only result in lowering the standards of private ethics and public taste. Perhaps Charles Francis Adams' judgment of rich men was a bit severe but not out of line with this stream of thought. "Not one that I have ever known," he wrote, "would I care to meet again, either in this world or the next; nor is one of them associated in my mind with the idea of humor, thought or refinement."[26] On this point at least American liberals could agree with the castigations of the contemporary rich by an English socialist.

> Jay Gould, the "financier," got more "pay" and held more wealth than Gladstone, and Carlyle, and Darwin, and Koch, and Galileo, and Columbus, and Cromwell, and Caxton, and Stephenson, and Washington, and Raphael, and Mozart, and Shakespeare, and Socrates, and Jesus Christ ever got amongst them.[27]

E. L. Godkin cited the worship of wealth and its "inevitably resulting corruption" as one of the basic dangers to democracy. Unchecked by either philosophy or religion, "it is breaking down, not simply the old political, but the old social usages and standards. The aristocratic contempt for money as compared with station and honor, of which we used to hear so much, has completely vanished."[28] And at the turn of the century Godkin wrote to *The Nation* that the greatest risk that came to every republic came "not so much from discontented soldiers as from discontented multi-millionaires."[29] His criticism is reminiscent of the trenchant observation of Wendell Phillips, "As usual in chemistry, the scum floats uppermost."[30]

In an age of wealth *The Nation* attacked the standards of wealth. It called it the "Age of Envy," for the spirit of envy infected the rich as well as the poor. "We are so set upon material ends," *The Nation* said in 1887, "that we exaggerate the importance of attaining them; and come to think little of success that does not 'materialize.'" It was

---

[26] Adams, *op. cit.*, p. 190.
[27] Robert Blatchford, *Merrie England: A Plain Exposition of Socialism* (New York: 1895), p. 139. Cited in Lecky, *op. cit.*, II, 502.
[28] Godkin, *Unforeseen Tendencies of Democracy*, pp. v-vi.
[29] *The Nation*, LXXI (1900), 362.
[30] Martyn, *op. cit.*, p. 582.

the sham of materialism that undermined character, distorted values, and obliterated that basic truth that "most suffering is the result of sin."[31] On another occasion, *The Nation* characterized post-Civil War America as a "Chromo-Civilization" of cheap and tawdry values.[32] The old liberal standards were being destroyed in the age of the worship of wealth.

> The popular hero to-day . . . is neither the saint, the sage, the scholar, the soldier, nor the statesman, but the successful stock-gambler. . . . And—what is worst of all—there is a growing tendency to believe that everybody is entitled to whatever he can buy, from the Presidency down to a street-railroad franchise.[33]

This attitude could not help but permeate all social and political as well as economic activities. The churches now catered to the gospel of wealth, and the daily press was too subservient to wealth to protest. Everywhere the tone of public life was falling under this corrupting influence. Cleveland, in the eyes of *The Nation*, stood out as the hero against this trend as he fought pensions, tariffs, and subsidies. But the heroes were few, and the times were against them. Educated men had long since withdrawn from public life, and now nothing was left but the bitter and often underhanded bargaining of the rich with the poor. Contrasted to Cleveland, the idol of the liberals, was Mark Hanna, whose career epitomized the spirit of the times. When liberalism had failed, Hanna was victorious, and with this triumph *The Nation* had little sympathy. After his death, *The Nation* summarized Mark Hanna's contribution to American politics:

> To invest money in politics as in a mine or railroad, and, to look as confidently for the pecuniary return; to appeal for votes on the basis of sheer material advantage; to cry up prosperity as the be-all and end-all of government; to vulgarize politics by making its watchwords the cries of the market and the slang of the gambler; to make of the electoral struggles of a free people an exciting game with huge and glittering money stakes—in a word, to put mercantile methods in the place of forensic, and to hold the best title to office to be the fact that it has been bought and paid for—this was the great political distinction of Mr. Hanna.[34]

Against the economic schemes of the poor and ignorant and the political and moral debauchery of the rich, *The Nation* waged a sustained and relentless struggle. However, when the issue came to a head in 1896 and Bryan in the name of the poor was matched against McKinley in the name of the rich, *The Nation* had no difficulty in choosing sides. It threw its support to McKinley.

Liberal democratic thought presupposed an enlightened electorate guided in their politics by recognized statesmen of character and edu-

[31] *The Nation*, XXXXV (1887), 432.
[32] *Ibid.*, XIX (1874), 201.
[33] *Ibid.*, XXXXII (1886), 419.
[34] *Ibid.*, LXXVIII (1904), 122-123.

cation. Rational men would weigh the characters of contending candidates in the scales of virtue and register a reasoned choice in favor of morality and learning. That such an optimistic picture was unlikely of realization was obvious to de Tocqueville, who noted that people in a democracy "not only seldom indulge in meditation, but they naturally entertain very little esteem for it."[35] The hurly-burly of an active life militated against contemplation, even of the problems of government. In time, John Stuart Mill came to the conclusion that with the imperfect system of education, "the ignorance and especially the selfishness and brutality of the mass," democracy would have to be modified in favor of a representative form of government.[36] The happy era of optimistic democracy seemed on the wane.

In the post-Civil War period the failure of the democracy to attract talented men into public service became a focal point for criticism of the American system. Bryce, in his *American Commonwealth*, devoted an entire chapter to the topic "Why the Best Men Do Not Go Into Politics." "The proportion of men of intellectual and social eminence who enter public life," he wrote, "is smaller in America than it has been during the present century in each of the free countries of Europe."[37] Lecky used this as a point of attack on democracies in general, and *The Nation's* reviewer tended to agree with him.[38] E. L. Godkin found that the "scholarly, thinking, philosophical class" spoke out too little and carried too little weight in the formation of public opinion. Gone were the Websters, Sumners, Marcys, Wrights, Sewards, Calhouns, Clays and Everetts. "The talent of the country in fact seems to have taken refuge in the great business corporations, and in the colleges, just as in the Middle Ages it took refuge in the monasteries."[39] The bosses, protectionists, and paternalists had taken over, and accordingly, "the thoughts of the *elite* of the nation naturally turn away from politics to fields in which a man may speak the thing he wills, and be the master of his own career."[40]

The educated classes had lost control as well as influence in America. To purify politics, and if possible, forestall too drastic a departure from the dreams of an earlier day, *The Nation* and the liberal movement it represented, turned to modifying the machinery of democracy. However, such modifications generally took the pattern of tending away from direct popular control. For the aim of the respectable reformers was to give to the virtuous and educated greater weight in political affairs than the "machines" permitted. Such statesmen would resist

---

[35] Alexis de Tocqueville, *Democracy in America* (New York: J. & H. G. Langley, 1843), II, 43.
[36] Mill, *op. cit.*, pp. 162, 133-134.
[37] Bryce, *op. cit.*, II, 65.
[38] Lecky, *op. cit.*, I, 114. *The Nation*, LXII (1896), 380-382.
[39] Godkin, *Problems of Modern Democracy*, pp. 211, 267, 306.
[40] *Ibid.*, p. 269.

the temptations of the cheap politicians and preserve democracy from the sins of paternalism and corruption. *Laissez faire* would thus be coupled with *noblesse oblige* as a last alternative of a failing democracy.

Between the good honest citizen and his government stood the "rings," bosses and machines. If these barriers could be removed or circumvented, honest men, it was felt, would return to government service, and men of talent to high places. James Bryce wrote,

> If the path to Congress and the State legislatures and the higher municipal offices were cleared of the stumbling-blocks and dirt heaps which now encumber it, cunningly placed there by the professional politicians, a great change would soon pass upon the composition of legislative bodies, and a new spirit be felt in the management of State and municipal as well as of national affairs.[41]

In this period American liberals set to work to remove the "stumbling-blocks and dirt heaps" that democracy might become respectable again. In the vanguard of this crusade for purity in politics was *The Nation* magazine. Its goal: retrenchment and reform.

As the basic reform issue of the times *The Nation* turned to the civil service. All other political reforms were of secondary importance compared to this. "No matter to what political reform we now turn our attention," it said in 1876, "we find the first step towards it must consist in a reform of the civil service."[42] George William Curtis, Carl Schurz, James Russell Lowell, all pressed for an extended merit system, but E. L. Godkin claimed for *The Nation* the credit for being the first periodical to take up this cause.[43] In 1867 *The Nation* pushed Mr. Jencks' civil service bill, "a bill that meets the evil which is at the bottom of our political Pandora's box." The bill would discourage incompetents from seeking government jobs and would open the door to qualified applicants who would "submit themselves honorably and decorously to the required examination."[44] Civil service reform would drive out of government sinecures that "enormous class of wire-pullers and managing men whose only idea of politics is to get a living out of the Government."[45] *The Nation* sought a classification system of grades and subdivisions with correlated pay and responsibilities which applicants could enter after passing satisfactorily a qualifying competitive examination. With graft, qualified men would not compete, but with intelligence, they would enter with alacrity. "Reform in the civil service," it declared, "must . . . be based on popular appreciation of the value of discipline, popular remembrance of the weaknesses of human nature, popular respect for law, and popular desire for excellence—that is popular love of seeing things well done. . . ."[46] As a reform move-

[41] Bryce, *op. cit.*, II, 71.
[43] *Ibid.*, LXXI (1900), 246.
[45] *Ibid.*, VIII (1869), 329.
[42] *The Nation*, XXII (1876), 241.
[44] *Ibid.*, IV (1867), 32.
[46] *Ibid.*, XV (1872), 294.

ment, it would have to be taken up by the people as the political bosses would resist it to the end. Year in and out *The Nation* sought to overthrow the bosses by going directly to the voters on this issue. No other reform was possible until the spoils system was eradicated. "Patronage controls conventions, conventions make nominations, the nominees control patronage, and so the circle is complete."[47] Here was the evil which underlay not only government inefficiency but community "moral rottenness." For it brought into the government "intrigue and hypocrisy, shamming, shirking, and corruption" and so made war on the "fundamental virtues of our civilization."[48]

The Nation hailed the Pendleton bill of 1883 as "the first retreating step on the downward road on which our administration entered when in 1820 the term of certain offices was limited to four years." Now at last the test of tenure in some offices would be good behavior, and there was the hope that the provisions of the act would be extended throughout the administrative branch. "We have in truth," *The Nation* wrote, "begun a process which ought to have been begun just sixty years ago. But it is only begun, and must be watched to completion."[49] *The Nation* watched, coaxed, cajoled, and entreated for a wider and more stringent application of the merit system. It praised Cleveland in 1889 mainly for his broadening of the merit system. "He has been one of the best Presidents we have ever had—a model of industry, an exemplar of honesty, a representative of common sense, and embodiment of courage...."[50] But E. L. Godkin, who guided *The Nation's* drive for the abolition of a spoils system that sapped the strength of government and polluted public offices, was not to see the reform completed in his time. Discouraged and depressed, he wrote to *The Nation* in 1900 that "Federal America is to-day, in the last resort, ruled by a small knot of 'bosses,' of the mental calibre and education of Platt."[51]

Writing in 1885 on its twentieth anniversary *The Nation* had been somewhat more optimistic about the cause of reform and its own part in it. As it looked back over its career, its opposition to Johnson's impeachment, carpet baggers, Grant's corruption, Greenbackers, and the spoils system, it felt it could say of itself with pride, "It has not been greatly wrong on any leading question of the last twenty years...." And of its learned and notable staff of contributors, "It is not too much to say that they will carry with them from this world the credit of having ... done something to hasten the coming of the better time, the reign of sweeter manners and purer laws."[52] For *The Nation* was not at heart an organ of complacency but an instrument for reform.

Carrying the principles of the merit system to the very steps of the White House, *The Nation* opposed Sumner's proposed amendment to

[47] *Ibid.*, XXXIII (1881), 46.
[48] *Ibid.*, XXXII (1881), 199.
[49] *Ibid.*, XXXVI (1883), 28.
[50] *Ibid.*, XXXXVIII (1889), 193.
[51] *Ibid.*, LXXI (1900), 247.
[52] *Ibid.*, XXXX (1885), 516-517.

the Constitution which would restrict the eligibility of the President to one term. Good behavior was still the proper test of tenure. And, it caustically reminded the Senator,

If the popular judgment needs to be put under constitutional restrictions with regard to Presidential re-eligibility, it certainly does in a tenfold greater degree with regard to senatorial re-eligibility, for while a bad President has never been re-elected, bad senators do somehow often get in for a second term.[53]

Whom are the people capable of electing, *The Nation* enquired, if they are not capable of determining the re-eligibility of so important a figure as the President?

In its quest for reform *The Nation* advocated an executive budget as early as 1882. To bring order out of the existing chaos of revenue and expenditure, it recommended "a complete budget of necessary expenditures, and of the taxation required to cover them, prepared by the executive branch of the Government and submitted to Congress at the beginning of each session."[54] Always a staunch supporter of the veto power of the President, as a check upon the popular passions, in 1886 it came out for the item veto of appropriation bills. This proposed amendment, reported unfavorably by the Judiciary Committee of the House, would achieve a salutary check upon Congressional log-rolling.[55] In 1885 *The Nation* urged administrative reorganization in Washington because of the continued growth of the many research bureaus.

By means of the merit system, judicious use of the President's power of removal, the indefinite eligibility of the President himself, the executive budget, the item veto, and administrative reorganization, *The Nation* hoped to see retrenchment in government achieved and efficiency realized. It sought to make the executive branch more effective, more economical, and accordingly, more responsible.

However, in time, as the Presidency developed strength and leadership under Theodore Roosevelt, *The Nation* became alarmed at a new trend. Now the people ran to the President "in childlike confidence, or else in weak dependence." We must guard against a new danger, *The Nation* cautioned:

We are coming to think of the Chief Executive as if he combined in himself the attributes of an Oriental King and a mediaeval monarch—as if he were a Solomon to decide all our controversies, and a Louis to decree righteous judgment from a "bed of justice."

This trend *The Nation* would resist as being "bad for him, and bad for us." It struck at self-help and Presidential efficiency at the same time. "Not tyranny, but corruption, is our most threatening foe," *The Nation*

[53] *Ibid.*, XIV (1872), 36.
[54] *Ibid.*, XXXV (1882), 106.
[55] *Ibid.*, XXXXII (1886), 350.

warned, "and there is no instrument of corruption like a President wielding the vast and abdicated powers of Congress in a way to suit the schemes of party bosses."[56]

While *The Nation* sought in the executive branch retrenchment and efficiency, it looked for deliberateness and learning in the legislature. Legislators should speak the wisdom of the community; they should have "familiarity with and confidence in the great principles of political science and the teachings of history."[57] Through reason, counsel and debate, bills ought to work their tedious path through legislative chambers to emerge in due course upon the statute books as models of precision, grammar, and utility, destined for long life. Demagogues and ignorant men worked in haste; the true legislator was known for his caution, prudence and learning. The failure of existing legislative bodies to approach this ideal led *The Nation* to recommend that legislatures be restricted in every conceivable manner, for "they constitute a part of the Government which we can best afford to abridge in its prerogative without at the same time striking at the root of popular liberty." Perhaps it was a bit of wishful thinking which led *The Nation* to say that "In all probability the world has already passed through the heyday of legislation. . . ."[58]

To reform the legislative branch *The Nation* advocated state legislative councils which would study all proposed legislation, recommend appropriate alterations, eliminate duplications and incongruities, and thus serve as a permanent and intelligent arm of the legislature.[59] Reason and deliberation would thus guard against hasty, ill-conceived legislation. For *The Nation* noted in 1895, "We suffer from two evils, the passion for framing new laws, and the willingness of Legislatures to act upon subjects which are not proper subjects of legislation at all."[60] All devices to expedite legislation and curtail debate were, therefore, opposed by *The Nation*. It attacked the hour rule in the House, and the use of the "previous question." "The action of deliberative bodies without talk causes far more mischief than their talk without action." Fearful of too much rather than too little government, it said, "It is far better that the representative should be bored by a long speech than that the constituency should suffer under a bad law."[61] By the interchange of ideas in free discussion over an indefinite period of time, true wisdom could be incorporated into law. It was once again the old liberal philosophy that among rational men untrammelled competition results in the triumph of good. The market place of the mind selected the true and the just, and rejected the false and unjust. To improve legislation, remove the barriers to free discussion.

[56] *Ibid.*, LXXIV (1902), 458.
[57] *Ibid.*, VII (1868), 126.
[58] *Ibid.*, XX (1875), 342.
[59] *Ibid.*, II (1866), 617; III (1866), 474.
[60] *Ibid.*, LXI (1895), 163.   [61] *Ibid.*, II (1866), 696, 697.

The Nation opposed the use of the "rules" of the House for partisan purposes, for this militated against free debate. What happens to a luckless independent who introduces a bill in the House?

The fate which overtakes him reminds one forcibly of that which befalls hogs in the great slaughterhouses. The last word is hardly out of his lips when "the rules" take hold of him and fling his resolution into the committeeroom, and shoot the author down a well-greased plank, at the bottom of which he is cut up and salted away in the densest obscurity and oblivion. . . .[62]

The Nation looked to a House modelled somewhat after the British House of Commons. The speaker should be a non-partisan officer who would protect the rights of minorities and independents as well as the majority. "If things go on as they are now going," it commented in 1890, "there will soon be no House of Representatives left, but merely a Speaker, a caucus, and a few chairmen of committees."[63]

In the Senate, The Nation fought the use of the unanimous consent device and that euphemism, "senatorial courtesy." It found the Senate in 1886 at the lowest point in its history.[64] Ten years earlier, The Nation had noted that the prestige of the Senate was on the decline due to its share and abuse of the appointing power of the President, the deterioration of State legislatures, the rise of powerful political machines, and the absence of any real political opposition.[65] By 1890 it could say, "The Senate has, in fact, become almost exclusively a capitalists' chamber. . . . At the North there is a steady tendency to give seats in it to successful manufacturers, speculators, or railroad men."[66] Gone were the noted lawyers, clergymen, and statesmen of earlier days, while the contemporary intellectuals were generally ignored.

The Nation was not of the belief that the evils of democracy could be cured by more democracy. The reforms it recommended usually tended in the opposite direction. However, the prevalent chaos and corruption which surrounded the State capitols at the time of the election of Senators, brought The Nation eventually around to the view that popular election could at least have no worse results, and it gave the direct election movement lukewarm support.[67]

The Nation believed in raising the level of democracy rather than broadening its base. It sought a more intelligent electorate rather than a more numerous one. It was for this reason that it shied away from the Negro suffrage movement and sought taxpayer qualification for voting in New York City. While it supported, at first, the woman suffrage movement, it soon turned away from this reform. It feared corruption resulting from sex. Legislative bodies, which had been so

[62] Ibid., XIV (1872), 316.
[63] Ibid., L (1890), 459.
[64] Ibid., XXXXIII (1886), 49.
[65] Ibid., XXII (1876), 222.
[66] Ibid., LI (1890), 4.
[67] Ibid., LXXIV (1902), 222.

easily corrupted in the past by money, would be subjected to "a deeper, and darker, corruption still." Just imagine, it cautioned with horror, the effect of the "female charms" upon our susceptible legislators. "Suppose this influence to be organized and systematized in the person of a large body of female members of Congress, and brought to bear on land-grants, subsidies, tariffs, charters, and public offices, what kind of thing would our legislation be?"[68] Obviously, there could be only one answer. Sex must be kept out of politics. Since "every female politician knows that she holds her male colleagues or opponents at her mercy," the possibilities for corruption far outweighed the possibilities for good.[69]

To break the bosses *The Nation* long advocated the Australian ballot and corrupt practices legislation which would outlaw bribery and intimidation and fully publicize campaign receipts and expenditures. It recommended adoption of proportional representation to give the intelligent minority some voice in legislative councils. To overthrow the caucuses and conventions *The Nation* advocated the direct primary method of nomination. With this adopted, the educated members of the community would at least have some opportunity to present a candidate, whereas heretofore they had been forced to choose between the corrupt caucus choices. However, it noted, a primary without state supervision would deliver the voter once again right back into the hands of the bosses.

The Nation spoke for the reformers on nearly all the current issues. At times it even went beyond most reformers as when it came out for the seating of Cabinet Officers in Congress[70] and amending away the "lame duck" session of Congress.[71] Nevertheless, the pattern of its ideas shows a desire to strengthen the existing democracy rather than to extend it. It sought not to extend the suffrage but rather to restrict and qualify it. It preferred an intelligent government from above, rather than an expanded government from below. Thus, it opposed the use of the referendum as tending toward a pure democracy. Faulty and corrupt as legislators were, they were still far more capable of governing than the vast majority of the people.[72]

As guardian of the nation's conscience, the Constitution, and the laws of classical political economy, *The Nation* would permit nothing to alter or in any way lower the position of the courts in our democracy.

---

[68] *Ibid.*, XII (1871), 271.

[69] *Ibid.*, XVII (1874), 312. *The Nation* felt that J. S. Mill's advocacy of woman's suffrage was based upon a lack of appreciation of the significance of sex. His *Autobiography*, it declared, revealed that Mills himself had no real understanding of the problem and that his "state of mind with regard to the relation of the sexes was essentially morbid, and that his experience of female character was narrow and onesided. . . ." *Ibid.*, p. 311.

[70] *Ibid.*, XXVIII (1879), 243; XXXII (1881), 107.

[71] *Ibid.*, XXXXV (1887), 452; XXXXVI (1888), 4.

[72] *Ibid.*, LVIII (1894), 206; LIX (1894), 152.

It sought to abolish in the states the elective judiciary which it felt brought second-rate men to the bench and tended to "overlook those quiet diligent, inobtrusive characters which are peculiarly the material out of which judges should be made."[73] The elective system tended to undermine the impartial administration of justice; therefore, "all the power of good men should be directed to a change in it."[74] The administration of justice was a field entirely separate from politics. Talk about the courts' being on the side of the rich against the poor was silly when not downright dangerous. "The courts and the law are on the side of both the poor and the rich so long as they obey the laws," *The Nation* said in the week of the Haymarket Riot.[75]

During reconstruction *The Nation* had disapproved of any interference by the Supreme Court. "All devices for protection against the will of a decided majority of the governing class are certain to fail; and nothing is more unwise than to thrust a few judges across the path which such a majority have resolved to pursue."[76] Now, however, that the majority had commenced a policy which involved government intervention in the economic sphere *The Nation* eagerly applauded each restrictive decision by the Court. The curtailment of railroad regulation, of the Anti-Trust Act and the overthrow of the income tax were all hailed as decisions which protected minority rights against a passionate majority.

Although *The Nation* opposed the extravagant use of the injunction by the courts in general, it always managed to defend its use in particular cases. Thus, it quoted with approval John M. Parker's statement, "Speaking for myself, I prefer a government by injunction to anarchy."[77] To *The Nation*, this, basically, was the only choice. Against all abuse, *The Nation* went loyally to the defense of the judiciary. When, finally, the Democrats in 1896 adopted a platform condemning the income tax decision, *The Nation* called it "The Platform of Revolution."

This blow at the courts shows how true are the instincts of the revolutionaries. They know their most formidable enemies. Judicial decisions have again and again drawn the fangs of confiscatory and revolutionary legislation, and the courts have come more and more to stand as the great bulwarks of property and personal right. It is perfectly natural, then, that men planning confiscation and revolution should strike hard at the chief obstacle in their way.[78]

As *The Nation* viewed the course of American politics after the Civil War, the increasing political strength of illiterate immigrants, radical reformers, and agrarian demagogues, the rise of Tweeds, Platts, Conklings, and the Goulds and Rockefellers, the declining political influence of Lowell and Norton and Curtis and Schurz, it felt America

[73] *Ibid.*, XVII (1873), 268.
[75] *Ibid.*, XXXXII (1886), 356.
[77] *Ibid.*, LXV (1897), 257.
[74] *Ibid.*, V (1867), 72.
[76] *Ibid.*, IV (1867), 394.
[78] *Ibid.*, LXII (1896), 62.

had entered upon a latter day decadence. Nominally an independent journal catering to the intelligent minority who would not be bound by party ties, it supported consistently the Republican presidential nomineees except when Grover Cleveland was a candidate. Cleveland, it felt, represented the ideals of the intellectuals.

The salvation of democracy must come with its recognition of the superiority of its intellectual leaders and the wisdom of abiding by their advice. Lowell had felt that "the highest privilege to which the majority of mankind can aspire is that of being governed by those wiser than they."[79] What, however, the intellectual leaders failed to understand fully was that America could no longer adhere to the early liberal ideal of a small government performing a minimum of functions. Failing thus, they failed as leaders, and their vitality was frequently dissipated by casting their most effective missiles at the wrong targets. They illustrated once again the truth in Wendell Phillips' pronouncement on the scholar in politics. "When common sense and the common people have stereotyped a principle into a statute, then bookmen come to explain how it was discovered and on what ground it rests."[80] The vanguard of the liberal movement of 1860 now found itself justifying ancient truths while new truths went on ahead. The words of Lord Morley on an English conservative, might now be applied to E. L. Godkin and the group he represented: "His ideal, like that of most literary thinkers on politics, was an aristocracy not of caste, but of education, virtue and public spirit . . . the old dream of lofty minds from Plato down to Turgot."[81]

The Nation in its oft-repeated plea for public recognition of the educated and enlightened expressed the hope not only that the wisdom of their teachings would be heard, but that character and virtue would find their proper place in the scheme of things. However, the goal of the intellectuals in education itself seems not to have been the inculcation of the inquisitive attitude so much as the indoctrination of a new generation with the standards of an old. Natural law in politics and economics had been revealed; all that was needed now was dissemination. Educated men with radical ideas were no fit leaders, nor were college professors who taught "ethical" economics more than corruptors of youth.

From 1865-1900 *The Nation's* primary reform in economics was tariff reduction; its primary reform in politics was the civil service. Beyond these, basically, it simply sought means of checking the popular passions, which it felt were largely manifestations of ignorance and sin. "The difficulty which a democracy has in conquering the passions,

[79] Lowell, *op. cit.*, VI, 29-30.
[80] Martyn, *op. cit.*, p. 576.
[81] Cited in Ernest Barker, *Political Thought: From Herbert Spencer to the Present Day* (New York: Henry Holt and Company, Home University Library Edition), p. 202.

and in subduing the exigencies of the moment, with a view to the future, is conspicuous in the most trivial occurrences in the United States."[82] Thus had de Tocqueville written, so now did *The Nation* write. Its early position in favor of the majority against the Supreme Court in reconstruction days was now reversed. Now it spoke the mind of the most conservative members of the Court. Justice David Brewer, nephew and direct intellectual descendant of Stephen J. Field, revealed a position which was not far from that of *The Nation* when he addressed the New York Bar Association in 1893:

> The Courts hold neither purse nor sword; they cannot corrupt nor arbitrarily control. They make no laws. They establish no policy, they never enter into the domain of public action. They do not govern. Their functions in relation to the State are limited to seeing that popular action does not trespass upon right and justice as it exists in written constitutions and natural law. So it is that the utmost power of the courts and judges works no interference with true liberty . . . it simply nails the Declaration of Independence, like Luther's theses against the indulgences upon the door of the Wittenberg church of human rights and dares the anarchist, the socialist, and every other assassin of liberty to blot out a single word.[83]

So to the courts, guardians of liberty according to natural law and conservative constitutional construction, did *The Nation* turn as the last stronghold of intelligent impartiality. "*Noblesse oblige* is a rule for nations as for individuals," Brewer informed Yale students in a lecture on citizenship.[84] With ignorance and corruption prevalent in the executive and legislative branches of government, *The Nation* would place this noble obligation on the courts. "In this country, having the courts to help us, what we do is to restrict the power of the legislature in every possible way," *The Nation's* reviewer said in endorsing Lecky's *Democracy and Liberty*.

Late nineteenth-century America exhibited to the liberals several basic social ills. The materialistic standards of the age militated against social preeminence because of manners and grace, and failed to accord due recognition to men of intellectual attainment. The balance of political power, it was felt, had shifted into the hands of the many ignorant and poor. This led to the tendency toward social legislation, which contravened the tenets of the liberal political economy. The struggle for power between the few rich and the many poor led to endless bribery, graft and corruption in general. To curb these regrettable proclivities of a democratic society, *The Nation*, like many others, turned to various forms of respectable reform. Though *The Nation* had not despaired

---

[82] De Tocqueville, *Democracy in America*, I, 249.
[83] New York Bar Association *Proceedings*, 1893, p. 46. Cited in Ralph Gabriel, *The Course of American Democratic Thought*, p. 233.
[84] David J. Brewer, *American Citizenship* (New York: Charles Scribner's Sons, 1902), p. 121.

of democracy, the criticism it voiced of democracy was the criticism as well of the English conservative opponents. "Lecky's remedy for the ills of Parliament and the dangerous tendency of democracy was, as in the case of Maine, 'machinery.' "[85] What Lippincott has written of the Victorian critics applies as well to *The Nation* and the class it represented. "Lecky's work showed conclusively that middle-class liberalism was not prepared to follow the logic implicit in its theories.... In rejecting economic democracy, liberalism rejected the means that would make political democracy truly significant."[86]

Many of the older American liberals thought that they saw democracy pass from a realized dream in 1865 to decadence in 1900. And not a few among them felt about America as C. F. Adams felt about the town of Quincy, Massachusetts. "The Quincy I knew has ceased to exist; and, with the present Quincy, I have neither ties nor sympathy."[87] However, *The Nation* pushed on for its reforms, still hopeful that the day would come when America would retrace its erring footsteps and return to the righteous path of old.

It may be said that the reforms *The Nation* advocated did not come to grips with the underlying socio-economic conditions that brought these problems into being, the conditions which made bosses and rings flourish in large cities, graft and corruption in state capitols and radical economic movements sprout out of the farmland. But in truth these reforms, the merit system, corrupt practices legislation, proportional representation, and the rest, were to serve civic leaders and political scientists as well for at least two generations to come.

[85] Lippincott, *op. cit.*, p. 243.
[86] *Loc. cit.*
[87] Adams, *op. cit.*, p. 204.

CHAPTER IV

PROGRESSIVISM: THE UNION OF POLITICS AND ECONOMICS

When Andrew Carnegie wrote *Triumphant Democracy*, he characterized the times as the high noon of the republic, "when the blazing sun right overhead casts no shadows." Within a decade the sun was to pass the meridian, and a new movement to be born in American politics, dedicated to removing the shadows and the stains on our political and economic life. Only a year after Carnegie revised his book, Henry Demarest Lloyd brought forth an attack on the system that produced Carnegies. It was an issue of *Wealth Against Commonwealth*, Lloyd declared. "As always happens in human institutions, after noon, power is stealing from the many to the few. Believing wealth to be good, the people believed the wealthy to be good."[1] As America was exposed to a new criticism in the next few years, as the techniques of wealth and political control were revealed, the sordid and the seamy were laid bare before the reading public, it became evident to many that the old political and economic formulas were no longer applicable to the present facts. The spirit of reform was in the air, but no longer was it predominantly that of the Cleveland-Mugwump-Brahmin variety.[2] The new spirit was based on new standards, reasoned from new theories, and sought new techniques. Those of the old liberals who could not make the adjustment to the new formulas and the new conditions were left with only their present sorrows and earlier dreams. "Our present political condition is repulsive to me," Godkin, now retired from *The Nation*, wrote at the turn of the century.

I came here fifty years ago with high and fond ideals about America, for I was brought up in the Mill-Grote school of radicals. They are now all shattered, and I have apparently to look elsewhere to keep even moderate hopes about the human race alive.[3]

To those who clung to the old formulas and "ancient truth," the old order had failed, and there was no promise in the new. To those not so restrained, progress and promise were at hand, not the automatic, mechanical progress of the Manchester liberals which resulted from negative government—but the social progress which resulted from a

[1] Henry Demarest Lloyd, *Wealth Against Commonwealth* (New York: Harper & Brothers Publishers, 1894), p. 515.
[2] John Chamberlain notes, "Cleveland, in the eighties and nineties, was the spearhead of a thrust that was less Democratic in the Jacksonian sense, than it was of the Manchester liberal brand." John Chamberlain, *Farewell to Reform* (New York: The John Day Company, 1933, 2nd ed.), p. 8.
[3] Ogden, *op. cit.*, II, 237.

positive government's social program. The current unrest gave promise of something new and something better. "It is not like the Granger episode or the Debs episode," A. J. Beveridge observed in 1906. "The former . . . affected only the farmers; the latter, only the workingmen. The present unrest, however, is quite as vigorous among the intellectuals, college men, university people, etc., as it is among the common people."[4] Here was a political movement out of middle-class America, safe from the extremes of conservative plutocracy and radical socialism, which could consolidate the forces of dissatisfied farmers, workers, and businessmen. It was natural, in fact inevitable, that this movement should contain the seed of twentieth-century liberalism.

As the plans and purposes of the progressive movement gradually unfolded, *The Nation*, reluctant to see rapid change, sided with the progress-awaiters against the progress-seekers. However, it did not wage any sustained war against the progressives; it merely trailed, far in the rear, the march of the times. The exposés and investigations had some effect. "Men who call themselves practical," *The Nation* noted in 1905,

are seriously asking whether wholesale debauchery of legislatures, boards of aldermen, and electorates is not too heavy a price even for so precious a boon as the largest insurance society on earth, the most extensive railway system, unlimited franchises for trolley lines, the most powerful lumber company, or the richest gold mine.[5]

The fight against debauchery *The Nation* could enter with vigor, for it was as dependable a foe of corruption as the preacher was of sin. But the positive progressive program it hardly understood and frequently when it did, met it with cold rebuke. The demand for municipal and state ownership of public utilities and more direct democracy it seldom coupled with the exposés. It failed to see that progressivism rose from fairly solid roots.

The impulses which gave it birth are, negatively, skepticism regarding the colorless scientific study of social science, and positively, an unreasoned feeling that if sympathy with the masses is only present, active work in their behalf will remove the doubts which settle on the old-fashioned student of politics and society.[6]

The progressives looked to positive government action to achieve reform; *The Nation* looked to individual action, a reaffirmation of ethical standards and more moral behavior. Its program looked to a free society in which the citizen would have "no tax to pay to the tariff baron . . . no graft to render to the politician . . . no obeisance to make

---

[4] Claude G. Bowers, *Beveridge and the Progressive Era* (New York: The Literary Guild, 1932), pp. 223-224.
[5] *The Nation*, LXXXI (1905), 159.
[6] *Ibid.*, LXXIX (1904), 69.

to the labor union, and . . . no enforced deference to his fellows who find their pleasure in mapping out the way to Utopia."[7] *The Nation's* approach was still the negative approach of the Manchester school. "If experience has not demonstrated," it cautioned the progressives, "that, when possible, it is best to limit the powers of Government rather than enlarge them, the lesson of history must be relearned."[8] In terms of basic approach, *The Nation* and the progressives were poles apart.

Opposed to Theodore Roosevelt, in 1904, *The Nation* happily endorsed Judge Parker. It wrote an editorial of relief when, in 1908, Roosevelt handed over the Presidency to Taft. For the sound and now conservative *Nation* felt ill at ease with the lusty Roosevelt in the White House. "His view of his duties is essentially jovial. He loves to slap the country on the back with a 'bright' thought," *The Nation* wrote in 1906. When Roosevelt proposed a progressive income tax to limit the amount of private fortunes *The Nation* passed it off as merely a hasty "happy-go-lucky remark." "It will be a mortification to his friends, and a real public misfortune, that his mouthing has made Bryan appear a reactionary, Hearst a conservative, and has elevated Debs and Powderly to the level of Presidential statesmanship." But *The Nation* felt that our institutions, Constitution, and conservative temperament would still save us from such "demagogues or improvisators."[9] When Roosevelt attacked the judiciary for a district court decision in the Beef Trust case, *The Nation* protested: "The authors of the Constitution surely never contemplated such a lecturing of the judges by the President; but then, it is probable that Hamilton and Madison would say that they never foresaw Roosevelt at all."[10] However, when he finally left office, though he had "given the country a long succession of shocks," *The Nation* was willing to award him due praise for the "solid achievements of his seven years in the Presidency."[11] With the issue, in 1908, between Taft and Bryan, *The Nation* sought to direct the independent vote to Taft. Here was a man the intellectuals could follow, a man of "judicial training." Furthermore, he represented the "less venal wing of the Republican party." Citing his qualifications *The Nation* noted:

The frankness of Mr. Taft's recent utterances in the matter of class legislation is decidedly in his favor. . . . He has not minced matters in reference to the boycott. He has come out boldly in defence of the equal rights of unorganized labor. He has scored the violence of strikers. He has stood up calmly and manfully for the integrity of the equity powers of the courts.[12]

If the independents thought they saw in Taft the makings of a second Cleveland, what they failed to see was that the Cleveland era of reforms was past. The new reformers would have nothing but progressivism.

[7] *Ibid.*
[8] *Loc. cit.*
[9] *The Nation*, LXXXII (1906), 314.
[10] *Ibid.*, p. 336.
[11] *Ibid.*, LXXXVIII (1909), 240, 241.
[12] *Ibid.*, LXXXVII (1908), 130.

When, in 1893, Frederick Jackson Turner made history at a meeting of the American Historical Association by pointing out "The Significance of the Frontier in American History," he hinted to the future historians at a new emphasis in historiography. "Steadily, the frontier of settlement advanced and carried with it individualism, democracy, and nationalism," read Turner.[13] Why was it that the frontier carried these concepts in its wake? Why did the frontier affect the course of American democratic development? Because, reasoned Turner, "So long as free land exists, the opportunity for a competency exists, and economic power secures political power."[14] Behind political forces and political systems were economic and social factors which, in the field of American history had scarcely been explored. To analyze politics, one must now delve into economics. Such an emphasis could hardly be considered novel; it was at least as old as Harrington, and more recently, had been popularized by Marx. American history, however, was still of the Bancroft, Oberholtzer and von Holst variety, and Turner performed a notable service toward making an economic emphasis respectable.

The older liberals, when they wrote of political economy, thought, in fact of two separate fields, politics and economics. Now that political science and economics had achieved the status of two separate disciplines, they became in substance reunited. Politics and economics were inextricably interwoven in the social order. Behind politics was economics; behind economics was politics. The Economic Man, and the Rational Man now faded out in the light of contemporary research.

While Turner and his followers went on to explore the influence of sectionalism in our history, the iconoclastic and solitary Thorstein Veblen cut through received economic theory into the wide and unexplored expanse of social analysis. *The Theory of the Leisure Class* (1899) and *The Theory of Business Enterprise* (1904), like his other writings, provided his few contemporary followers and his many disciples of the next generation with a new technique and a new vocabulary. Economic theory and practice were to Veblen not rational, but institutional. The Veblen vocabulary of conspicuous consumption, waste, and leisure, pecuniary emulation, predatory habits, and the instinct of workmanship testifies to the cultural implications of his research. *The Nation*, however, gave scant encouragement to Veblen. Its reviewer passed off *The Theory of Business Enterprise* with the observation that

Such a theory . . . may impress the readers of sensational magazines; but it is a travesty of economics, and an unjust aspersion of our business morality. It may affect the imagination of the half-educated by its ponderous

[13] Frederick Jackson Turner, *The Frontier in American History* (New York: Henry Holt & Company, 1921), p. 35.
[14] *Ibid.*, p. 32.

platitudes, its obscure and complicated presentation of simple ideas, even by the barbarisms of the author's style.[15]

Clearly, to *The Nation* at least, the distinction between workmanship and predatory behavior was an invidious one. Veblen's discussion of the standards of taste and the nature of emulation in a pecuniary society cast a new light on economic behavior and business morality. If this was heresy to the orthodox in the progressive era, it served as gospel to a new generation of economic theorists.[16]

While Veblen wove his web of heterodoxy about the cherished standards and beliefs of early twentieth-century America, a political scientist, J. Allen Smith, scrutinized the sacred symbol of American society, the Constitution of the United States. In 1907 *The Spirit of American Government* appeared. Its title was innocuous enough, unless one noticed its sub-title, *A Study of the Constitution: Its Origin, Influence and Relations to Democracy.* For Smith was not writing a eulogy of the founding fathers and the Constitution they created. Rather was it his purpose to call to the attention of progressive America "the spirit of the Constitution, its inherent opposition to democracy, the obstacles, which it has placed in the way of majority rule. . . ."[17] Taking as his fundamental thesis the view that responsible government needs no checks, that the check and balance system was originally developed to restrain irresponsible rulers, he vigorously assaulted the heretofore glorified American Constitution. "The system of checks and balances must not be confused with democracy; it is opposed to and can not be reconciled with the theory of popular government."[18] Under the guise of democracy the Constitution, a reactionary curtailment of popular gov-

---

[15] *The Nation*, LXXXI (1905), 38. When Joseph Dorfman brought out *Thorstein Veblen and His America* in 1934 (New York: The Viking Press), *The Nation's* reviewer (H. B. Parkes) said Veblen was "the most penetrating and realistic of American sociologists." Only Marx had excelled Veblen in his insight into capitalism. "Veblen without Marx is apt, therefore, to result in a rather futile liberalism. Read in conjunction with Marx, however, he remains a singularly wise and far-seeing thinker." In America, the reviewer added, "Veblen's books are probably the most congenial introduction to the revolutionary attitude." *The Nation*, CXLI (1935), 194-195.

[16] John Chamberlain wrote in 1934, "Veblen is more than Veblen. When Messrs. Berle and Means write on 'The Modern Corporation and Private Property,' they are developing aspects of Veblen's thought. . . . When John T. Flynn traces the complex of evils flowing from periodic overcapitalization, he is corroborating an insight that was old to Veblen in 1912." New York *Times*, November 27, 1934, p. 19. R. L. Duffus declared that "the influence of Thorstein Veblen's thinking will outlast that of any economist, perhaps any sociologist, of his generation." New York *Times*, December 2, 1934, V, 5. Walton Hamilton has acknowledged the debt of contemporary economists to Veblen, and Max Lerner has said of Veblen's work that "it encompasses the most important body of social analysis in modern American thought." See Max Lerner, *Ideas Are Weapons* (New York: The Viking Press, 1939), pp. 128, 125. Among contemporary political economists there seems to be no end of acknowledged indebtedness to Veblen.

[17] J. Allen Smith, *The Spirit of American Government* (New York: The Macmillan Company, 1907), p. vii.

[18] *Ibid.*, p. 9.

ernment, had been foisted upon the public. The Framers were not far-sighted self-abnegating patriots. Rather, was it their object to bind and restrict popular, majority rule in as many instances as possible. "They represented ... the wealthy and conservative classes, and had for the most part but little sympathy with the popular theory of government."[19] The Framers at the Convention felt that "the less the people had to do with the government the better."[20] Democracy was "the very thing which they wished to avoid."[21] Why were the Framers fearful of majority rule? Because they represented property interests and were eager to protect property rights. "The chief danger which they saw in the Revolutionary state governments was the opportunity afforded to the majority to legislate upon matters which the well-to-do classes wished to place beyond the reach of popular interference."[22]

Thus, by going back to the Constitutional Convention, Smith pointed up a basic conflict in American politics; the conflict between property rights and popular rule. Contrary to current misconceptions, Smith declared, the Framers represented the side of the former against the latter.

The Constitution was in form a political document, but its significance was mainly economic. It was the outcome of an organized movement on the part of a class to surround themselves with legal and constitutional guarantees which would check the tendency toward democratic legislation.[23]

It was because this conflict had been resolved in Convention on the side of the property interests that subsequent popular movements generally ran afoul of the Constitution. And the heavy hand of the Framers lay over the progressive movement. "In the United States at the present time," wrote Smith, "we are trying to make an undemocratic Constitution the vehicle of democratic rule."[24]

To question the source of the revelation of 1787, to deny that the Constitution had simply frozen into organic law the basic principles of the Declaration of Independence, was, in effect, to remove the halo of divinity which history had placed about the names of the founding fathers. This was more than sophisticated muckraking; it was the unfolding of a new interpretation of political history which placed its emphasis upon economics. *The Nation's* reviewer called it "scientific Bryanism" and dispensed with its author with the observation that "He has no understanding of the true democracy, which aims at once at the liberty of the individual, as also of the masses. And this liberty consists in resting the power of government in the more abiding national consciousness."[25] The exact location of the "more abiding national consciousness" was not revealed.

[19] *Ibid.*, p. 32.
[21] *Ibid.*, p. 30.
[23] *Ibid.*, p. 299.
[25] *The Nation*, LXXXV (1907), 121.
[20] *Ibid.*, p. 37.
[22] *Ibid.*, pp. 297-298.
[24] *Ibid.*, p. 31.

The new interpretation of history, however, would not be put down. Some six years later, Charles A. Beard documented and elaborated Smith's thesis.[26] The title itself was brazen: *An Economic Interpretation of the Constitution of the United States*. Basing his study on what he called the "political science of James Madison," he pursued an approach suggested in the *Federalist*, No. 10. "Those who hold and those who are without property have ever formed distinct interests in society," Madison had written. Now Beard developed and made specific this approach in hope that contemporary historians would "turn away from barren 'political' history to a study of the real economic forces which condition great movements in politics."[27] The economic interpretation showed vested interests to be vitally concerned with checking popular rule. The founding fathers spoke not for human rights but for "money, public securities, manufactures, and trade and shipping." "The Constitution," wrote Beard, "was essentially an economic document based upon the concept that the fundamental private rights of property are anterior to government and morally beyond the reach of popular majorities."[28]

Smith's study had, apparently, little influence; Beard's work, however, caught hold. This academic exposé not only posited a theory, but carefully documented it with a tabulation of the property and political beliefs held by the members at the Convention. The economic emphasis caught the spirit of progressivism.[29] Max Lerner has observed that the significance of Beard's study lay in its new evaluation of basic assumptions.

The premise even of the muckrakers had been of an original Eden, and a fall from grace—to be remedied by the atonement of reform. But Beard laid bare the basic struggle between democracy and capitalism and traced it back to the origins of the American state. Eden had never been Eden.

The basic conflict that took place in 1787 thus had contemporary significance. "The triumph of the oligarchs that Beard's contemporaries were witnessing was thus not contrary to the spirit of 1789 but a logical culmination of it."[30]

[26] Beard acknowledged indebtedness to Turner in his Introduction, though he gave only a footnote reference to Smith.
[27] Charles A. Beard, *An Economic Interpretation of the Constitution of the United States* (New York: The Macmillan Company, 1914), p. v.
[28] *Ibid.*, p. 325.
[29] John Chamberlain relates a story which illustrates the conservative reaction to Beard's work. Nicholas Murray Butler when President of Columbia is reported to have answered the question, "Have you read Beard's last book?" with the terse reply, "I hope so." Chamberlain, *op. cit.*, p. 210.
[30] Lerner, *op. cit.*, p. 160. Chamberlain wrote, "In the light of Charles A. Beard and J. Allen Smith, it becomes doubly evident that the Progressivism of 1902-1912 was mainly an attempt to over-ride the spirit of the Constitution, and return to the Declaration of Independence; and to recreate the Constitution in the interests of the people...." Chamberlain, *op. cit.*, pp. 213-214.

The Nation's reviewer gave fair though brief notice to *An Economic Interpretation of the Constitution*. Its suppressed ire was released, however, in an editorial of 1915 entitled "Muckraking the Fathers."
If the American Revolution was fought for land-grabbing and crooked finance, if the Protestant Revolution was merely an expropriation of the Church, if the French Revolution was an assault on ecclesiastical revenues, what will prevent the historian of the year 2050 from describing the social uplift movement of 1915 as primarily engineered by young men and young women of the middle classes in search of jobs as investigators and research directors, and the socialist party as made up of lazy factory hands, grafting walking delegates, and ambitious lawyers.[31]

The scholars, Turner, Veblen, Smith and Beard showed the influence of economic circumstances on political and social behavior. Economic theory could no longer be considered separate and apart from politics. While the scholars quietly rewrote history in accordance with an economic interpretation, the muckrakers made history sensational and brought it up to date. Gustavus Myers wrote a *History of the Great American Fortunes*, Ida Tarbell expanded Lloyd's study in her *History of the Standard Oil Company*, while David Graham Phillips exposed *The Treason of the Senate*. There were many others, but basically the theme of all the muckrakers was the same: politics and economics were gripped together and economics held the upper hand. No longer was the big businessman the paragon of character and success in the Spencerian sense. Lincoln Steffens checked the major cities and always ran across the trail of the big businessman. "I found him buying boodlers in St. Louis, defending grafters in Minneapolis, originating corruption in Pittsburgh, sharing with bosses in Philadelphia, deploring reform in Chicago, and beating good government with corruption funds in New York."[32] The *laissez faire* conception of negative government had done a fair job of keeping government out of business; it had failed, however, to keep business out of government.

America had heretofore operated on a double standard. It had assumed that its politicians were easily corrupted and thus must be hedged and checked at every turn. Only its judges were above suspicion, and these only when appointed. With equal conviction the presumption was in favor of the businessman. His character and ethics

---

The editor of *New Republic* took a poll of leading "educators, historians, critics, lecturers or publicists" in 1938 to find out what books "had affected their own ideas." The response is of interest. "In the letters taken as a whole the titles that recurred most frequently were 'An Economic Interpretation of the Constitution' and 'The Theory of the Leisure Class' . . . ." See Malcolm Cowley and Bernard Smith, *Books That Changed Our Minds* (New York: Doubleday, Doran & Company, Inc., 1939), pp. 19-21.

[31] *The Nation*, C (1915), 72.

[32] Lincoln Steffins, *The Shame of the Cities* (New York: McClure, Phillips & Co., 1904), p. 5.

were generally above reproach. "Business ethics" were thus the antithesis of "political corruption." Now the muckrakers sailed into business behavior and found not all as "ethical" as originally supposed. Politicians were hedged about with constitutional restraints to keep them from doing serious harm to society. Yet, under *laissez faire*, what were the restraints on harmful business activity? Corruption and graft were exposed in the Equitable Insurance Company, the Pennsylvania Railroad, Standard Oil, and elsewhere. "This is the ugly thing," *The Nation* wrote in 1906. "The disease which we have complacently assumed to be confined to politicians, we now see infecting business men." It came as a revelation to *The Nation*. "We have too easily concluded that graft and favoritism and methods that would not bear the light are the vices of politicians." The progressive program looked to various forms of government regulation of business. *The Nation's* program, however, remained that of its earlier days. "Our only hope is in a quickened conscience and a moral toning-up all round."[33]

If economic factors controlled political development, if the most influential of the economic forces, big business, frequently employed corrupt practices, then there could be little political or economic liberty for the average middle-class American unless the government intervened directly in the economic sphere to correct obvious abuses. The progressives now sought, by various means, to make economic power responsive to political control, to make big business responsible to government, and government in turn more directly responsible to the people.[34]

In 1912 Walter Weyl wrote *The New Democracy*, in which he expressed much of the spirit and program of progressivism. "The new spirit is social," Weyl pointed out. "It emphasizes social rather than private ethics, social rather than individual responsibility."[35] The war against the modern plutocracy was social rather than individualistic in its implications. "It is this social interpretation of rights which characterizes the democracy coming into being, and makes it different in kind from the so-called individualistic democracy of Jefferson and Jackson."[36] J. Allen Smith had observed that "The control exerted over the individual directly by the government, may, as a matter of fact, be slight in comparison with that which is exercised through the various agencies which control the economic system."[37] Now Weyl found that "the chief restrictions upon liberty are economic, not legal, and the chief prerogatives desired are economic, not political."[38]

[33] *The Nation*, LXXXII (1906), 440.
[34] It is perhaps ironical that often the supporters of the thesis that economic power determines political control have also advocated extending political control in order to check economic power.
[35] Walter E. Weyl, *The New Democracy* (New York: The Macmillan Company, 1912), p. 160.
[36] *Ibid.*, pp. 161-162.   [37] Smith, *op. cit.*, p. 305.   [38] Weyl, *op. cit.*, p. 164.

To protect society against plutocracy and to expand individual liberty, Weyl presented a program which included a range of political and economic reforms, from government ownership of utilities, government competition with and regulation of business, to the extended use of the initiative, referendum and recall. He would make business responsible to the government, and the government responsible to the people. Positive government action need not restrict freedom, Weyl noted, but may actually enlarge it.

A law forbidding a woman to work in the textile mills at night is a law increasing rather than restricting *her* liberty, simply because it takes from the employer *his* former right to compel her through sheer economic pressure to work at night when she would prefer to work by day. So a law against adulteration of food products increases the economic liberty of food purchasers, as a tenement house law increases the liberty of tenement dwellers.[39]

Walter Lippmann took to shattering idols and ridiculing taboos in his *Preface to Politics*. Seeking a more dynamic approach to politics, he struck at eighteenth-century mechanism and the so-called impartiality of the law. "The law," he quoted from Anatole France, "in its majestic equality forbids the rich as well as the poor to sleep in the streets and to steal bread." What was needed was a more positive approach to existing social conditions. The old negative government approach was no longer realistic. "It is perfectly true that that government is best which governs least," wrote the enigmatic Lippmann. "It is equally true that that government is best which provides most. The first truth belongs to the Eighteenth Century; the second to the Twentieth."[40] The state should be regarded not as an instrument of repression but as a "creator of opportunities." The old standards had passed away, Lippmann wrote shortly afterward:

The dominant forces in our world are not the sacredness of property, nor the intellectual leadership of the priest; they are not the divinity of the constitution, the glory of industrial push, Victorian sentiment, New England respectability, the Republican Party, or John D. Rockefeller.[41]

The search for new standards and new techniques led away from the traditional belief in individualism and negative government. The old promise of American life, wrote Herbert Croly in 1909 was a "mixture of optimism, fatalism, and conservatism."[42] Today, however, "The sincere and candid reformer can no longer consider the national Promise

---
[39] *Loc. cit.*
[40] Walter Lippmann, *A Preface to Politics* (New York and London: Mitchell Kennerly, 1914), p. 266.
[41] Walter Lippmann, *Drift and Mastery* (New York: Mitchell Kennerly, 1914), p. xviii.
[42] Herbert Croly, *The Promise of American Life* (New York: The Macmillan Company, 1911), p. 5.

as destined to automatic fulfillment."⁴³ To assure its fulfillment, positive government action was required. Under the old system,

> with its assumption of a substantial identity between the individual and the public interest . . . unusually energetic and unscrupulous men were bound to seize a kind and an amount of political and economic power which was not entirely wholesome.⁴⁴

To redress matters what was now needed was a nationalized reform. "The new Federalism or rather new Nationalism is not in any way inimical to democracy," Croly declared. On the contrary, it would "give a new meaning to popular government by endowing it with larger powers, more positive responsibilities, and a better faith in human excellence."⁴⁵ Progressivism was shifting the American emphasis from individual rights to social responsibilities, from the the state to the national level of government, and from the negative conception of government as a policeman, to the positive conception of government as provider and regulator.

The Nation had sympathy with the progressive movement to the extent that progressivism meant cleaning up corruption, reforming the civil service, and reducing the tariff; in other words, as long as progressivism seemed an instrument for realizing the old ideals. When the insurgent Republicans broke with the regulars over the tariff issue in 1910, *The Nation* hailed the event as a "manifestation of returning health" to the Republican party. "All signs point to the opening of a new chapter in the party's history."⁴⁶

As the scope of the progressive program became apparent, however, *The Nation* became skeptical. The duty of the true political leader in these disturbing times, *The Nation* said, "is to draw a clear line between public ills that are remediable by legislation and those that are not." Once again it voiced its ancient fear of excessive legislation.

> The quack doctors of politics . . . have a law to propose for every trouble. . . . But the honest practitioner will tell the truth about the ills to which mortals have always been subject, and always will be so long as they live in communities, and will advise the necessary endurance of those, with as much patience as may be, while the attention is given to what need not be endured because it can be cured.⁴⁷

The great political question of the times was where to draw the line between ills that could be cured by legislation and those that could not. It was here that *The Nation* differed with progressives and turned against them. The progressives looked to greater political control over economic activity and more direct, democratic control in politics. *The*

⁴³ Croly, *op. cit.*, p. 20.
⁴⁵ *Ibid.*, pp. 169, 170.
⁴⁷ *Ibid.*, XCI (1910), 205.
⁴⁴ *Ibid.*, p. 149.
⁴⁶ *The Nation*, XC (1910), 394.

Nation was traditionally opposed to both. "Common to all the progressive schools is the assumption that there is a people that must be freed," it wrote in 1912. "It is not an enslaved citizenship that we have had, but in the largest measure an independent people."[48] The voices of progressivism, however, spoke otherwise. "Freedom to-day is something more than being let alone," Woodrow Wilson declared in 1912. "The program of a government of freedom must in these days be positive, not negative merely."[49]

In 1910, Theodore Roosevelt, back from his hunting expedition in Africa, struck out for more domestic prey. The audience at Osawatomie, Kansas, John Brown territory, heard the Bull Moose take his stand. "I stand for the square deal," he declared, but ". . . I mean not merely that I stand for fair play under the present rules of the game, but that I stand for having those rules changed so as to work for a more substantial equality of opportunity and reward." The old individualistic conceptions of the unlimited private rights of property must now give way to the new view that "every man holds his property subject to the general right of the community to regulate its use to whatever degree the public welfare may require it." Following the line of thought developed by Croly, Roosevelt went on to demand a "New Nationalism without which we cannot hope to deal with new problems." The program was, once again, one of positive government, emphasizing social needs as opposed to private rights. "The betterment which we seek must be accomplished, I believe, mainly through the national government." The new program meant, of course, "far more governmental interference with social and economic conditions than we have yet had, but I think we have got to face the fact that such increase is now necessary." To achieve these purposes, Roosevelt looked to making the Presidency "the steward of the public welfare."[50]

Such a program was anathema to *The Nation* and it speedily attacked "this half-baked Rooseveltian Socialism." The thought of extending so drastically the powers of government and raising the Presidency to "the infallible righter of all economic wrongs" was indeed shocking. "The great question," *The Nation* wrote, "is whether or not the old-time American sturdiness and common sense have still sufficient vitality to throw off this pseudo-socialist virus before it has done immeasurable mischief."[51]

In Columbus, Ohio, in 1912, Roosevelt complemented his economic program with his ideas for political reforms. "I believe in pure democ-

---

[48] *Ibid.*, XCIV (1912), 508.
[49] Woodrow Wilson, *The New Freedom* (New York: Doubleday, Page & Company, 1921), p. 284.
[50] Henry F. Pringle, *Theodore Roosevelt* (New York: Harcourt, Brace and Company, 1931), pp. 542-543.
[51] *The Nation*, XCI (1910), 233.

racy," he now said, ". . . that human rights are supreme over all other rights . . . that wealth should be the servant, not the master, of the people." To approach this pure democracy he sought extended use of the initiative, referendum and recall, the latter even to apply to state judicial decisions on constitutional questions.[52] This last feature struck at the foundation of *The Nation's* position, for this would deprive the judiciary of their present happy impartiality.

As among Taft, Roosevelt and Wilson, in 1912, *The Nation* chose Wilson. Taft represented the old guard, high tariff interests. Roosevelt was entirely unacceptable.[53] Woodrow Wilson, however, represented the old liberal ideal of the scholar in politics, and *The Nation* endorsed him "as a living embodiment of hostility to boss rule, as particularly well fitted to lead the battle against tariff abuses and all forms of privilege. . . ." Here, at last, was "a high-toned Democrat."[54]

In theory at least, the Wilsonian approach was not far distant from the old liberalism. "The New Freedom," Wilson said, "is only the old revived and clothed in the unconquerable strength of modern America."[55] He attacked bossism, high tariffs and privilege. "The government, which was designed for the people, has got into the hands of bosses and their employers, the special interests. An invisible empire has been set up above the forms of democracy."[56] This, too, was *The Nation's* battle. "What I am interested in," said Wilson, "is having the government of the United States more concerned about human rights than about property rights."[57] This was progressivism. However, the Wilson program looked toward restoring competition and letting competition regulate economic activity. The Roosevelt program, on the contrary, looked to permitting monopoly, but regulating it. Wilson stressed the state level of government, while Roosevelt turned to the national level. William Allen White chided that the difference between the programs of Roosevelt and Wilson was the difference between Tweedledee and Tweedledum. To *The Nation*, however, the difference was basic.

Wilson and the Democratic party plant themselves firmly on the ground of progress, of relief, of reform, of improvement, by measures that will curb monopoly, revive legitimate competition by repressing unfair and oppressive competition, and preserve the ancient freedom and self-dependence of Ameri-

[52] Pringle, *op. cit.*, pp. 557-558.
[53] Writing on Taft's defeat in 1912 *The Nation* observed, "Placed in the White House by grace of Theodore Roosevelt, he is now expelled from it by revenge of Theodore Roosevelt." (XCV [1912], 421). Its obituary of the Progressive party it saved until 1916. Then it said that, though the movement contained many sincere people, "the party was, in its essence, a movement for political revenge; . . . it tied its fortunes to the tail of one man's kite; and . . . when he fell it was bound to go down also." *The Nation*, CII (1916), 688.
[54] *Ibid.*, XCIV (1912), 582.
[55] Wilson, *op. cit.*, p. viii.
[56] *Ibid.*, p. 35.
[57] *Loc. cit.*

can citizens. Between this position and that of the Rooseveltians there is a deep gulf fixed. But between the position of the Rooseveltians and a full-fledged socialistic state, taking under its wing all the economic activities of the nation, and leaving no standing ground for individual self-assertion and development, no man can erect any substantial barrier.[58]

Throughout the progressive movement *The Nation* held fairly fast to its faith in the old liberalism. It attacked subsidies, tariffs, and political corruption as ever. But it, too, was swept along somewhat with the temper of the times. It saw the need of pure food and drug legislation, but would have preferred to see this handled by the states. It saw the need of labor legislation to protect women and children in factories, but this again was a state concern. Federal child labor laws, "would be a precedent of almost boundless potency for the assertion, as occasion may present itself, of Federal authority over one department after another of the life of the people of the several States."[59] It attacked the railroad rebate system, but feared the granting of rate-fixing powers to the Interstate Commerce Commission. It opposed the trusts more vigorously than before, but applied the "rule of reason" and did not see the need for the Clayton and Federal Trade Commission acts. It strongly opposed the labor union exemption in the Clayton Act. It eventually went along with the income tax amendment, but felt the tax should be levied at a uniform rather than a progressive rate. "With the rule of a uniform rate abandoned, there is absolutely no principle that can serve as a guide."[60] *The Nation* protested the discrimination against the Negro, and it attacked the "grandfather clause" and discriminatory city ordinances. It favored the direct election of Senators; this method could produce no worse results than the old. It favored, as before, the short ballot and the direct primary, while continuing to be dubious of the initiative and referendum. It looked toward stricter corrupt practices legislation, limiting the expenditures of money in elections and outlawing contributions from corporations. It opposed legislation curtailing the equity powers of the courts in labor disputes, the recall of judges or judicial decisions, and the appointment of Brandeis to the Supreme Court. Had not Brandeis been opposed by "eminent Boston lawyers and the six most recent presidents of the American Bar Association?" In proper indignation *The Nation* declared, "It is unseemly that a judge should enter the Supreme Court by the door of passion and political wrangling."[61] The Congressional struggle over the rules in the House of Representatives caught *The Nation* in an inconsistency. Formerly, it had attacked the rules, limited debate, the committee system and the extraordinary power of the Speaker. Now it defended the system.

[58] *The Nation*, XCV (1912), 204.
[59] *Ibid.*, XCVIII (1914), 151.
[60] *Ibid.*, XCVI (1913), 432.
[61] *Ibid.*, CII (1916), 506.

The rules of the House are not arbitrarily devised green withes wherewith to bind the young Samsons of statesmanship. For each of them, there is a reason, and it is a reason growing out of the needs of the public business, orderly conducted, and of party government, duly in control of legislation.

"Aside from what is offensive in Mr. Cannon as Speaker," it thus announced, "the recent outcry against the rules of the House seems to us largely ill-judged."[62]

The Nation took no positive part in the progressive movement. As a critical journal of contemporary opinion, speaking for the intellectuals, its criticism registered a protest against the spirit of progressivism rather than a willingness to lead or guide it. Its faith, the old liberalism, was not the faith of the progressives. Intellectual progressives like Weyl and Lippmann found, after 1914, an outlet in Croly's *New Republic*, whose editors *The Nation* later characterized as subscribing to the view "that an ounce of fresh experiment is worth at least a pound of experience, and that the day after tomorrow is better than a thousand yesterdays."[63] For its part, *The Nation* now preferred what was, in effect, a tempered conservatism, and its voice was that of scholars and school teachers rather than realists.[64]

In the turbulent election year of 1912, *The Nation* said:

We can easily understand why fastidious minds should shrink from the rude contacts and the rough voices of our great political contests. Why those whose faith in the democratic movement is growing cold should also dread the committing of such great issues to so vast an electorate, we can also understand.

But, quoth the school teacher, "The Presidential election may be conceived of as a kind of national examination. How are the pupils in the

[62] *Ibid.*, LXXXVIII (1909), 268.
[63] *Ibid.*, CIV (1917), 410.
[64] Undoubtedly, *The Nation's* attitude toward the progressive movement was colored partially by the editorship of Paul Elmer More from 1909-1914. Mr. More is associated in American letters with so-called Neo-Humanism, which on its socio-political side emphasized the doctrine of the élite, inequality of men and the sanctity of private property. "Why should there not be an outspoken class consciousness among those who are in the advance of civilization as well as among those who are in the rear?" More has written. (See Robert Shafer, *Paul Elmer More* (New Haven: Yale University Press, 1935), p. 203. In his *Shelburne Essays* More has made such statements as: "To the civilized man *the rights of property are more important than the right to life*." "The dollar is more than the man. . . ." (See "Aristocracy and Justice" in *Shelburne Essays*, Ninth Series (Boston: Houghton, Mifflin Company, 1915), pp. 136, 141. More's sympathetic biographer stresses More's fear of the "externalization of life at the expense of personal responsibility, and the relapse of the individual to barbarism." Following More, his biographer writes: "We have to be always on our guard against a veritable army, or rabble, of zealous bureaucrats, narrowly trained experts, professional reformers, plausible charlatans, flattering demagogues, blackguards of the daily and weekly press, self-appointed censors, and bigots, all of whom would persuade us, for the greatest variety of reasons, to extend without limit the scope and functions of government." (See Shafer, *op. cit.*, p. 201.)

school of democracy getting on?"[65] The virile *Nation* had, in fact, grown prissy. It directed its talents against the new school of realism in criticism and politics. In 1915 it wrote

Our staff of contributors, selected in the main, from the academic world throughout the country, have a peculiar opportunity just at this moment. The scholar's discipline, directed by well-tried principles, may yet make the sway of the great god Change less easy.[66]

In the age of progress and social responsibility *The Nation* urged conservatism and individual responsibility and countered materialism with idealism. In 1916, it noted that,

Even now a preoccupation with economics has led many to place the blame for human wreckage mainly upon external circumstances, that is, upon environment. . . . The modern equivalent of Nemesis—failure resulting from defects in character—has received all too little attention; yet unless it is taken into account, well-meaning reforms bid fair to defeat themselves by uprooting some of men's best instincts; in especial the sense of personal responsibility, however humble and harassing the conditions encountered.[67]

Now *The Nation*, quite properly, advertised itself as being the "organ of thinking people, the exponent of sane progress, of wise Conservatism."[68]

[65] *The Nation*, XCIV (1912), 150.
[66] *Ibid.*, CI (1915), 34.
[67] *Ibid.*, CIII (1916), following page 606.
[68] *Ibid.*, CII (1916). See "Supplement to *The Nation*," June 29, 1916.

CHAPTER V

LITTLE AMERICA AND PACIFIST LIBERALISM

Peace, retrenchment and reform epitomized the politics of the Gladstone, Mill and Bright school of English liberalism. These were also the goals of the American disciples of this liberalism. This was true especially of *The Nation* under the editorship of E. L. Godkin, which lasted till the turn of the century. Godkin, A. V. Dicey noted, "accepted the political creed of the mid-Victorian era in its wisest and in its noblest form. He accepted the maxim then adopted by almost every Liberal, that the object of rational government should be the attainment of 'peace, retrenchment, and reform.' "[1] While not a pacifist, Godkin nevertheless seemed to believe that among rational men there need be no war. Disagreements could be settled equitably by proper and timely recourse to arbitration. The brotherhood of man could approach realization through a commercial cosmopolitanism brought about by universal free trade. Free trade was the pathway to peace. "They are," wrote Richard Cobden in 1842, "one and the same cause."[2] The *laissez faire* demand for a minimum of government intervention in the internal affairs of the country carried over into the international field as well. For the logic of *laissez faire* was equally applicable to either field. Individuals could determine and pursue their own self-interest best with a minimum of restrictions, and intervention led to favoritism and mercantilism. "I am against any interference by the government of one country in the affairs of another nation," Cobden wrote in 1858, "even if it be confined to moral suasion."[3] Always in the background of the old liberal line of thought was a distrust of government which manifested itself at every turn. People are peaceful; if they are let alone, wars will not occur. Wars result from the machinations of misguided governments; therefore, government should never be entrusted with too much power for it may be used oppressively at home or abroad. Wars, *The Nation* wrote in 1904 in the light of the Spanish-American, Boer, and Russian wars,

are made not by people, but by diplomats. They spring not from race jealousies or international hatreds, but from the negotiations, the exigencies, too often from the diseased pride or the political ambitions, of Foreign Secretary or President.[4]

By the turn of the century, however, the old liberalism had quite lost its hold, both here and in England. The liberalism that had sup-

[1] *The Nation*, CI (1915), 52.
[2] J. A. Hobson, *Richard Cobden* (London: T. Fisher Unwin, Ltd., 1918), p. 37.
[3] *Ibid.*, p. 400.
[4] *The Nation*, LXXIX (1904), 288.

planted mercantilism proved powerless before imperialism. "In the politics of the world, Liberalism is a declining almost a defunct force," *The Nation* observed in 1900. "Only a remnant, old men for the most part, still uphold the Liberal doctrine, and when they are gone, it will have no champions."[5] In May, 1902, one of the most outspoken of the remnant, E. L. Godkin, passed away. In its obituary, *The Nation* fittingly recited of its former editor:

> He grow old in an age he condemned,
> Felt the dissolving throes
> Of a social order he loved,
> And, like the Theban seer,
> Died in his enemies' day.[6]

The new imperialism was a political-economic movement of many causes, reflecting diverse aspirations. Economically, it expressed the demand for new outlets for investment capital, raw materials for hungry factories, and new markets for finished goods. Politically, it represented the culmination of nineteenth-century nationalism, the desire to be among the fittest that survived. It was, in all, the fairly logical result of centrifugal economics and centripetal politics in a world made smaller by revolutionary inventions in transportation, communication and business techniques. Combining missionary zeal with political-economic astuteness, imperialism became for America a movement with momentum, coupling selfish desires with altruistic aspirations.

Josiah Strong caught the spark of late nineteenth-century American imperialism when he wrote a little volume for the Home Missionary Society in 1885, entitled *Our Country*. The mission of the Anglo-Saxon, Strong felt, was to Christianize and civilize the world, for he was "divinely commissioned to be, in a peculiar sense, his brother's keeper."[7] Over a decade before either the Spanish-American or Boer wars, Strong divined the future of the race. "Does it not look," he observed,

> as if God were not only preparing in our Anglo-Saxon civilization the die with which to stamp the peoples of the earth, but as if he were also massing behind that die the mighty power with which to press it?[8]

Commercialism, Christianity, and Darwinian biology were woven into the same pattern in Strong's thinking and proved to him the glowing prophecy of America's mission:

> If I read not amiss, this powerful race will move down upon Mexico, down upon Central and South America, out upon the islands of the sea, over upon

---

[5] *Ibid.*, LXI (1900), 105.
[6] *Ibid.*, LXXIV (1902), 404.
[7] Josiah Strong, *Our Country: Its Possible Future and Its Present Crisis* (New York: Baker & Taylor, 1885), p. 161.
[8] *Ibid.*, p. 165.

Africa and beyond. And can any one doubt that the result of this competition of races will be the "survival of the fittest?"[9]

In such a manner would the Anglo-Saxon, "unless devitalized by alcohol and tobacco," become the master race and destroy the dreaded evils of barbarism, Catholicism and socialism.

No less an imperialist, but with a different emphasis, was Alfred T. Mahan. The Reverend Mr. Strong sought to spread the faith; Captain Mahan sought national security through the acquisition of strategic outposts safeguarded by an expanded navy. A naval strategist, Mahan emphasized *realpolitik*, and gauged the temper of the age of imperialism. "Communities which want and cannot have, except by force, will take by force, unless they are restrained by force," he noted.[10] In an early and important article in the *Atlantic Monthly* (December, 1890), Mahan wrote of "The United States Looking Outward." The old days of isolation and disarmament were over and, irresistibly, a new age had come to pass. "Whether they will or not," Mahan declared, "Americans must now begin to look outward. The growing production of the country demands it. An increasing volume of public sentiment demands it."[11] Though there were commercial benefits to be had by "looking outward," primarily Mahan's thesis turned upon the twin requirements of national defense: naval outposts and capital ships. With these secured, America itself would be secure against all hostile contingencies.

Every danger of a military character to which the United States is exposed can be met best outside her own territory—at sea. Preparedness for naval war—preparedness against naval attack and for naval offence—is preparedness for anything that is likely to occur.[12]

Thus, what was politically and economically a good offense, became, via Mahan, strategically the best of all defenses.

No more eloquent a champion of American imperialism existed, perhaps, than A. J. Beveridge. He took the buoyant logic of the cause and spread it broadcast in flamboyant language. When the Spanish-American war had ended, he demanded the retention of the conquered territory as, in an Indianapolis address, he hailed "The March of the Flag." He told of the virtues of "McKinley the Just," and spoke of the Philippines as the "noble land that God has given us." The Spanish-American war he characterized as

the most holy ever waged by one nation against another—a war for civilization, a war for a permanent peace, a war which, under God, although we knew it not, swung open to the republic the portals of the commerce of the world.

[9] *Ibid.*, p. 175.
[10] Captain A. T. Mahan, *The Interest of America in Sea Power, Present and Future* (Boston: Little, Brown, and Company, 1917), p. 253.
[11] *Ibid.*, pp. 21-22.
[12] *Ibid.*, p. 214.

The liberal's demand for self-government for the new territories he ridiculed. "It would be like giving a razor to a babe and telling it to shave itself." To the argument that Cuba, Porto Rico, Hawaii and the Philippines should be cast off because they were non-contiguous territories, he replied, "Our navy will make them contiguous." America could no longer resist the challenge of the times. "We must find new markets for our produce, new occupation for our capital, new work for our labor." As Beveridge discerned, "God's great purposes," he summed up the thoughts of many native imperialists when he solemnly concluded, "Fellow Americans, we are God's chosen people."[13]

Imperialism was anathema to *The Nation*. While others were looking outward, *The Nation* and the liberal remnant looked backward to the ideals of political liberty and self-government. "If John Stuart Mill or Charles Sumner could return to this world," *The Nation* wrote in 1905, "he would be simply bewildered by the radical change in political thinking. To talk of human rights as a political datum, or even as a political end, is supposed today to be the mark of a speculative Rip Van Winkle." Imperialism was the very antithesis of peace, retrenchment and reform. "It means immense outlay, war not peace, privilege not equality. All the philosophic disguises that may be invented cannot conceal the facts."[14] That such a doctrine should mask behind the theory of the survival of the fittest was purely pernicious. Though *The Nation* had supported social Darwinism as applied to domestic commercial life, it now discovered the flaw in it when applied to international politics. For if the goal of the expansionists is achieved, "it will indeed be in accordance with evolution; but if it is defeated it will just as much be in accordance with evolution, and evolution of a much more satisfactory kind."[15]

The Nation stood for international morality in an age of power politics and loyalty to conscience in an age of blind patriotism. It decried "that doctrine of devils and of fools 'Our Country, Right or Wrong,'"[16] and looked back upon the American faith of an earlier generation. "Anti-Imperialism is only another name for old-fashioned Americanism," it wrote in 1902.[17] Its Americanism was the Americanism of the 1870's; the newer manifestation was hardly intelligible to *The Nation*.

"Americanism" . . . is a distinct reversion to archaic and barbarous forms of feeling and action. It calls for passionate and sudden action. It contemns and distrusts and impedes deliberation. It associates consideration for the feelings or interests of others with cowardice and want of patriotism. It

[13] A. J. Beveridge, "The March of the Flag." *Modern Eloquence* (Philadelphia: John D. Morris and Company, 1903), XI, 224-242.
[14] *The Nation*, LXXXI (1905), 159, 160.
[15] *Ibid.*, LXVI (1898), 455.
[16] *Ibid.*, LXXIII (1901), 201.
[17] *Ibid.*, LXXIV (1902), 361.

makes national happiness and prosperity dependent on foreign misery and calamity. It tries to excite envy by exhibitions of brute strength. It covers weakness with ridicule. It minimizes and ignores domestic evils and abuses. . . .[18]

The imperialists talked about the American destiny; *The Nation* and the "little Americans" talked about the American tradition.

In order to combat more effectively the political sway of "manifest destiny," the liberals turned to the establishment of the Anti-Imperialist League. Originating in Boston, home of the anti-slavery movement, Anti-imperialist leagues were formed in a dozen cities by the end of 1900. Active members included E. L. Godkin, C. F. Adams, Grover Cleveland, Senator Hoar, C. E. Norton, Carl Schurz, Andrew Carnegie, David Starr Jordan, and William Graham Sumner. For the most part, the anti-imperialists did not carry on their campaign on the basis of constitutional or even economic considerations, but rather based their arguments "almost exclusively on grounds of abstract political principle."

They opposed it because they thought that an imperialist policy ran counter to the political doctrines of the Declaration of Independence, Washington's Farewell Address, and Lincoln's Gettysburg Address—the doctrines which asserted that a government could not rule peoples without their consent, and that the United States, having been conceived as an instrument of and for its own people, should not imitate the methods or interfere in the affairs of the Old World nations in any way.[19]

Grover Cleveland attacked the imperialists' conception of the mission of America, and announced to the Associated Press in 1898 that "The mission of our nation is to build up and make a greater country out of what we have, instead of annexing islands."[20] Senator George F. Hoar, who had supported the annexation of Hawaii, now opposed the movement to take in the Philippines and struck out at the new patriotism. "A man who would use an appeal to the flag in aid of the subjugation of an unwilling people," he declared, "would be capable of using the sacramental wine for a debauch."[21] With some relish Hoar relayed to his fellow Republicans "Pitchfork" Ben Tillman's caustic barb. "Your slogans of the past—brotherhood of man and fatherhood of God—have gone glimmering down through the ages. The brotherhood of man exists no longer."[22]

In Cambridge, in June, 1898, Charles Eliot Norton addressed the Men's Club of the Prospect Street Congregational Church on "True

[18] *Ibid.*, LVI (1893), 137.
[19] Fred H. Harrington, "The Anti-Imperialist Movement in the United States, 1898-1900," *The Mississippi Valley Historical Review*, XXII (1935), 211-212.
[20] Allan Nevins (ed.), *Letters of Grover Cleveland* (Boston: Houghton, Mifflin Company, 1933), p. 492.
[21] George F. Hoar, *Autobiography of Seventy Years* (New York: Charles Scribner's Sons, 1903), II, 320.
[22] *Ibid.*, p. 305.

Patriotism." He reminded his audience that "A declaration of war does not change the moral law" and sought to tone down the passions of the hour. His own great distress was evident:

My friends, America has been compelled against the will of all her wisest and best to enter into a path of darkness and peril. Against their will she has been forced to turn back from the way of civilization to the way of barbarism, to renounce for the time her own ideals.[23]

And, later that month, Norton confided to a friend his fears for America's future.

The old America, the America of our hopes and our dreams has come to an end, and a new America is entering on the false course which has been tried so often and which has often led to calamity. This war will in the long run result in far more evil to the United States than to Spain.[24]

Carl Schurz wrote articles and delivered speeches to do his bit against the imperialist movement. In the *Century Magazine* of September, 1898, he attacked those who found expansionism to be the Divinely inspired mission of America. "The American people may well pause before accepting a counsel which, in seeking to unload upon Providence the responsibility for schemes of reckless ambition involving a palpable breach of faith, falls little short of downright blasphemy."[25] So highly did Andrew Carnegie esteem Carl Schurz's work that he was happy to finance the publication of at least one of Schurz's anti-imperialist speeches. "You have brains and I have dollars," Carnegie wrote to Schurz. "I can devote some of my dollars to spreading your brains." Carnegie felt, in 1898, that the majority of the people were opposed to imperialism and that only the folly of the leaders had brought about the imbroglio. "Do not lose faith in the republic or in Triumphant Democracy," he wrote to Schurz. "It is sound to the core."[26]

When Carl Schurz was invited to deliver the Convocation Address at the University of Chicago in January, 1899, he selected as his topic "The Issue of Imperialism." In this rather lengthy speech Schurz answered, point by point, the arguments of the imperialists. Still, the central theme emphasized fidelity to the basic American ideals, for in this manner would we do our greatest service to our fellow men.

We can exercise the most beneficent influences upon mankind, not by forcing our rule or our goods upon others that are weak by the force of bayonets and artillery, but through the moral power of our example, by proving how the greatest as well as the smallest nation can carry on the government of

[23] C. E. Norton, *Letters of Charles Eliot Norton* (Boston: Houghton, Mifflin Company, 1913), II, 266, 268-269.
[24] *Ibid.*, p. 273.
[25] Frederic Bancroft (ed.), *Speeches, Correspondence and Political Papers of Carl Schurz* (New York: G. P. Putnam's Sons, 1913), V, 512.
[26] *Ibid.*, p. 531.

the people by the people and for the people in justice, liberty, order and peace without large armies and navies.[27]

While Godkin, Norton, and Schurz attacked the expansionists on the basis of peace, equality, and self-government, David Starr Jordan condemned war on the basis of scientific evidence. War did not result in the survival of the fittest, wrote Jordan, but rather in the survival of the unfit. "If a nation sends forth the best it breeds to destruction, the second best will take their vacant places. The weak, the vicious, the unthrifty will propagate, and in default of better will have the land to themselves."[28] Thus was the decay of the race brought about and the collapse of empires.

So fell Greece and Rome, Carthage and Egypt, the Arabs and the Moors, because, their warriors dying, the nation bred real men no more. The man of the strong arm and the quick eye gave place to the slave, the pariah, the man with the hoe, whose lot changes not with the change of dynasties.[29]

While Jordan attacked imperialism from Leland Stanford, William Graham Sumner carried on the fight from Yale. Sumner scoffed at the great ambition to be a world power. "A world power," he wrote in his *Folkways*, "is a state which expects to have a share in the settlement of every clash of interests and collision of state policies which occurs anywhere on the globe."[30] He too looked back to the days when self-government and individual liberty were considered something sacred. "What will come of the mixture of sentimental social philosophy and warlike policy?" he inquired. "There is only one thing rationally to be expected, and that is a frightful effusion of blood in revolution and war in the century now opening."[31] When Sumner died in 1910, *The Nation* extended "a warm and hearty appreciation of the service he rendered to his country during our war with Spain and in the Philippines. . . ."

His pamphlet, "The Conquest of the United States by Spain," is unanswerable in its logic, and must remain notable in that literature of patriotic protests against national error, which, through all our history, has so often been justified with the lapse of time. Wedded to the faiths of the fathers of this country, by no specious argument of temporal advantage could he be made blind to the lasting spiritual and moral losses which departure from those traditions involved.[32]

[27] *Ibid.*, VI, 20-21.
[28] David Starr Jordan, *The Blood of the Nation* (Boston: American Unitarian Association, 1906), pp. 21-22.
[29] *Ibid.*, p. 57.
[30] William Graham Sumner, *Folkways* (Boston: Ginn and Company, 1906), p. 63.
[31] William Graham Sumner, *War and Other Essays* (New Haven: Yale University Press, 1911), p. 30.
[32] *The Nation*, XC (1910), 395.

The Spanish-American war and its Philippine aftermath made a complete pacifist out of at least one newspaperman, Oswald Garrison Villard, later editor of *The Nation*. This conversion was to have a decided effect upon the course of *The Nation's* future policies.[33]

Opposed as it was to the imperialist movement, *The Nation* resisted each new manifestation of the jingo spirit. It broke, temporarily, with Cleveland over the Venezuela affair and attacked Olney's extension of the Monroe Doctrine. It opposed the plan to annex Hawaii because "the American republic, based upon the doctrine that all governments derive their just powers from the consent of the governed, proposes to change the government of a distant country without asking the consent of the governed in any way whatever."[34] It opposed the Spanish-American war as being entirely avoidable and the subsequent acquisitions of Spanish dependencies as being contrary to our historic principles. It opposed the abrupt method by which we acquired the Panama Canal.

At one stroke . . . President Roosevelt and Secretary Hay have thrown American principles to the winds and have committed the country to a policy which is ignoble beyond words. . . . It is the most ignominious thing we know of in the annals of American diplomacy.[35]

With acquisition a *fait accompli*, *The Nation* turned its efforts to a long and determined campaign to secure independence for the Philippines. To this end it envisaged an agreement among the Great Powers to guarantee the neutrality of the Philippines in the same manner as Switzerland was neutralized. Such an agreement, *The Nation* felt, would check the argument of those who maintained that if we withdrew, Germany or Japan would move in.

Best of all, it can be said for the neutralizing plan that it would be an act of justice, relieve us from the expense and worry of maintaining troops, forts, and fleets to guard them, and enable the Filipinos to begin to govern themselves at once, free from interference, no matter how many times they may stumble and fall before they learn to stand on their feet.[36]

[33] Oswald Garrison Villard, *Fighting Years* (New York: Harcourt, Brace and Company, 1939), p. 100.
[34] *The Nation*, LXV (1897), 410.
[35] *Ibid.*, LXXVII (1903), 374. "To show how scrupulously correct was our own conduct throughout, we need to read only the telegrams laid before Congress. Why, we did not recognize the revolution a minute before it occurred! In our supreme desire to follow the right course in stealing a canal, we telegraphed our consul at Panama on November 3 to find out if there was a revolution for us to recognize. He promptly replied that there was none yet, but hoped there would be in the course of the night. So, with great forbearance, our Government waited—with some impatience, it is true, but still it waited. Then note also how absolutely proper we were in paying no attention to Colombia's protest against our shearing off her best province. That protest did not arrive in Washington, Secretary Hay carefully observes, until two hours and fifteen minutes after we had recognized the independence of Panama. Of course, it was then too late to do anything. Justice might have required us to act, but think of the bad form!" See *ibid.*, p. 395.
[36] *Ibid.*, LXXXII (1906), 48. See also: LXXXV (1907), 249.

The Nation posited an international community composed of free nations pursuing rational foreign policies in an interdependent harmonious world. It adopted in international affairs the *laissez faire* assumption of a harmony of interests. Without the improper intervention of government, rational men throughout the world would walk the pathway of peace, bound in harmonious union by the practice of free trade. Because it found the basic interests of all men the same, it felt that any incidental conflicts might be resolved by the simple expedient of arbitration. Recourse to war was, after all, a barbaric means of settling disputes, and furthermore, did not necessarily achieve justice.

As an instrument for the settlement of international controversies upon the principles of reason and justice in place of force, *The Nation* strongly endorsed the Hague Conference of 1899 and the Court of Arbitration it established. "There is such a thing as an international conscience," *The Nation* said in 1899, and it looked forward to the day when all international disputes would be settled in international tribunals.[37] However, it noted that merely to establish a Court of Arbitration was going only half the distance. "No two countries which wanted to arbitrate ever had much difficulty in forming a court. The great difficulty is in agreeing to refer the question in dispute to arbitrators, not in finding the arbitrators." Thus *The Nation* pressed for the conclusion of agreements between nations to submit future disputes to the Court for settlement.[38]

Shortly after the creation of the Court of Arbitration, *The Nation* extended its own program to go beyond the settlement of disputes by arbitration alone. It now looked to judicial settlement rather than arbitration. By 1904, *The Nation* was writing that, "If individuals submit to the decision of the court of justice, associations of individuals can do so." It thus would transpose into the realm of international affairs certain basic concepts of municipal law. "It is immaterial that these associations are called nations; or rather it is all the more material that these great communities should take the final step in the advance of civilization which began with the suppression of private war."[39]

The Nation hoped that the Second Hague Conference might devise such a system for the judicial settlement of international disputes. "Civilization has called upon man to give up being judges in their own cause, and to surrender the right of private vengeance," it wrote in 1907. The real problem before the Peace Congress and the Hague Conference is whether an arrangement cannot be devised whereby a peaceful settlement of difficulties will be made as compulsory and satisfactory between nations as it has been between the citizens of each nation.[40]

[37] *Ibid.*, LXVIII (1899), 368.
[38] *Ibid.*, p. 410.
[39] *Ibid.*, LXXVIII (1904), 508.
[40] *Ibid.*, LXXXIV (1907), 352.

When the Conference ended, however, and *The Nation* surveyed its accomplishments, it regretfully concluded that "Taking the work at The Hague as a whole . . . it cannot be denied that it is a keen disappointment."[41]

Believing in peace as a universal program for rational men, and believing that the thorniest conflicts were capable of amicable judicial settlement reenforced by the conscience of mankind, *The Nation* consistently opposed large armament programs as instrumentalities of unnecessary wars and fought doggedly for international disarmament. At this time it was not pacifistic; it supported coastal defenses and armaments, but it opposed armaments for aggression. Rather than an extensive armament program for defense *The Nation* relied upon the avoidance of war and a "fuller recognition of international good faith and conscience."[42] Rather than promoting peace, armament races only promoted rivalry. "Peace does not depend upon fear. It goes with good will and mutual respect." To preserve peace *The Nation* urged a quickening of the international conscience rather than an increase in armies and navies. "War is a game which kings would not play if their subjects were wise," *The Nation* said.

It is the duty of those who make and unmake statesmen—namely, the people who have to pay the taxes and furnish their bodies as food for cannon—to insist by voice and pen and vote that war, and the huge armaments that lead to war shall be kept out of their thoughts and plans.[43]

Throughout the imperialist era, an age of petty wars, of land-grabbing, armament races, intervention and subjugation, *The Nation* stood for peace, arbitration or judicial settlement, non-intervention, disarmament, and self-government. It was an optimistic, idealistic program. But what *The Nation* assumed as "given," was hardly "given." It assumed peace-loving peoples who abhorred militarism, the desirability of universal free trade to achieve maximum economic advantage to all, a harmonious community of free and equal nations and an international citizenry of rational and ethical men whose patriotism gave vent to logic instead of emotion. Thus the span ever widened between *The Nation's* ought-to-be and the realities of everyday power politics.

In politics all evils demand a scapegoat. Whereas in domestic politics, *The Nation* had indicted the common man for the failures of democracy, in international affairs it found its scapegoat in the statesmen and placed its faith in the ever peace-loving people.

Writing in the Fall of 1913 in condemnation of the imperialistic doctrine of Anglo-Saxon superiority, *The Nation* observed that, though there was a cultural affinity between the United States and England which precluded war between them, "It is still true that war between

[41] *Ibid.*, LXXXV (1907), 366.
[42] *Ibid.*, XCIII (1911), 437.
[43] *Ibid.*, LXXIX (1904), 288-289.

this nation and any other of the leading Powers of Europe is almost equally inconceivable." "Does any statesman really foresee the chance of our engaging in hostilities with the German Empire, or with Russia, or with France?" it went on to inquire. No, *The Nation* answered.

The old arguments still hold. Situated here on the Western Continent, at a remote distance from the age-old rivalries that make of Europe an armed camp, these United States are as unlikely to be the armed enemies of one European country as of any other.[44]

Beyond Anglo-Saxondom, between friends as well as enemies, stood the Atlantic Ocean, undiminished in size since Washington, Monroe, or, in fact, the elderly Mahan. Within a year the status of this ocean was to play a decisive role in political thinking.

When World War I broke out, *The Nation* was quick to condemn the Kaiser and German militarism. "By this action Germany has shown herself ready to lift an outlaw hand against the whole of Western Europe," it wrote of the invasion of neutral Belgium, and entitled its article "The Responsibility for War."[45] The blame lay not against the German people, but the makers of war—the militaristic statesmen. "Out of the ashes," *The Nation* said, "must come a new Germany, in which democracy shall rule, in which no one man and no group of professional man-killers shall have the power to plunge the whole world into mourning."[46] Although pro-allied, *The Nation* at this time sought to preserve and protect our neutrality. It took issue with England for offending our rights as neutrals on the sea. "No plea of extreme necessity, or of life or death for England or any other Power, can avail to set aside the indefeasible rights of neutrals at sea."[47] More sacred than survival of the contestants were the rights of neutrals. It severely rebuked Germany for its announcement of a war zone off England in which neutral ships might be sent to the bottom.

If this is not braggadocio, it is brutality. It is also arrant stupidity, for, if it were not held to be sheer piracy, it would be an act of war against neutrals—or, at least, an act which, if not instantly apologized for, with an indemnity offered, would lead straight to war.[48]

Applicable as the concept of neutrality may have been in previous wars, the World War, involving as it did a magnitude of forces, human and economic, whose effects were felt around the globe, made any form of neutrality precarious if possible at all. No longer was a preponderance of force in the hands of the neutral powers who might assert their rights against a few minor contestants. International law, descending from previous customs and conventions, declared the rights of neutral states; the political and economic interdependence of states in

[44] *Ibid.*, XCVII (1913), 204, 205.
[46] *Ibid.*, XCIX (1914), 182.
[48] *Ibid.*, p. 156.
[45] *Ibid.*, XCIX (1914), 151.
[47] *Ibid.*, C (1915), 5.

the twentieth century placed uncertain reality ahead of accepted law. From a legal point of view, the rights of neutrals in the Crimean War were equally applicable in the World War; from a political-economic point of view these rights were subject to re-evaluation in terms of the Irishman's grim jest: "Neutral against whom?"

As Woodrow Wilson completed his second year in office *The Nation* reviewed his term and passed favorable judgment. "His conduct of the Government throughout the whole crisis of the European war has been such as to win the steadily widening approval and confidence of his fellow-countrymen." And it added prophetically, "It may even be that fate has in reserve for him a great part in the final settlement of the war."[49] When Senator La Follette attacked our policy of supplying the Allies with weapons of war as a violation of our neutrality, *The Nation* showed little sympathy for the special protectors of our neutrality. What sort of neutrality would be represented by ceasing this practice in the midst of the war, it asked. "In what other way," it sarcastically inquired, "than by thus suddenly throwing whichever party may happen to be profiting more from that practice upon his own resources could you give him so clear a demonstration of real neutrality?"[50]

The difference between the German and English violations of American neutrality were, in 1915, generally held to be that the Germans destroyed American lives while the English destroyed property. To *The Nation* the distinction was more than this. American lives could be saved if Americans refused to travel on the high seas until the termination of the war; but this *The Nation* opposed.

The bottom fact in the case is that, unlike matters relating to contraband, or blockade, this right is so simple and elementary, and has been so wholly free from challenge for generations, that to violate it, strikes at the very root of international faith, and to defend it without reserve or qualification is a prime duty of national self-respect.[51]

However, in the matter of property rights, we indeed had violated these during the Civil War—if improper, at least there was precedent. *The Nation's* neutrality was clearly pro-Allied.

Uncertain of Hughes, whom, as a conservative, *The Nation* would have preferred to support, it urged the re-election of Woodrow Wilson. It had complaints enough of Wilson, but, it wrote shortly before the election of 1916, "In the supreme testing of the past two years he has met, we believe, the supreme wish of the American people. He has striven to uphold the national dignity and honor. He has striven for peace."[52]

As the war continued *The Nation* leaned closer to the Allied side and further away from neutrality. It had early placed the responsibility

---

[49] *Ibid.*, p. 266.
[51] *Ibid.*, p. 373.
[50] *Ibid.*, CI (1915), 371.
[52] *Ibid.*, CIII (1916), 389.

for the war on Germany. In 1916 it observed that this war was forced on the Allies. "They did not seek it. The outside world thinks to-day that it was forced upon them, and we firmly believe that the verdict of history will be that this opinion is correct."[53] When Germany announced the renewal of unrestricted submarine warfare in February, 1917, and Wilson severed diplomatic relations with her, *The Nation* supported Wilson as taking the only possible course. "Having begun the European war by an act of perfidy, the German Government now seeks to end it by an act of criminal insanity."[54] Yet it urged the American people to remain calm and not to rush into militarism and war. "But if war should come, it is certain that the Government could count upon all the volunteers whom it could train and equip."[55]

Though *The Nation* approved of our diplomatic course of action, it strongly opposed conscription as a means of implementing this. Preparedness, it felt, would lead to war, and consistent with its former policies, it continued to resist radical increases in the army or navy. In the fall of 1916 *The Nation* presented its analysis of conscription in which it found: "(1) that it is utterly un-American in its every tendency; (2) that it would be a menace to our democratic institutions; (3) that it is practically unworkable; (4) that it is totally unnecessary."[56]

Nevertheless, when Wilson went before Congress and asked for the arming of merchant ships, *The Nation* supported Wilson and armed neutrality, and had no use for the La Follette filibusters. "The arming is merely against an evil day which may not come," it said hopefully.[57] A month later, the United States declared war. *The Nation* wrote of that momentous event:

All told, Americans may take deep satisfaction in the fact that they enter the war only after the display of the greatest patience by the Government, only after grievous and repeated wrongs, and upon the highest possible grounds.[58]

In January, 1918, *The Nation* announced the "voluntary retirement" of its fifth editor, Harold DeWolf Fuller, and the assumption of editorial control by its owner, Oswald Garrison Villard.[59] Thus was the quiet conflict of the last three years, between the pacifist owner and the pro-war staff, resolved. While *The Nation* had drifted from pro-Allied neutrality into war, Villard himself had held fast to his pacifism. In 1914, when the war began, Villard founded a "League to Limit Armaments," because, he explained, "there was an immediate outcry

[53] *Ibid.*, p. 531.
[54] *Ibid.*, CIV (1917), 150.
[55] *Ibid.*, p. 151.
[56] *Ibid.*, CIII (1916), 601.
[57] *Ibid.*, CIV (1917), 228.
[58] *Ibid.*, p. 388.
[59] Villard, *op. cit.*, p. 348. "Mr. Fuller left *The Nation* because he found himself no longer in sympathy with the restrained war policies of the paper. . . ."

from our jingos and militarists that we must follow in Germany's footsteps and militarize."[60] He marched in peace parades, spoke out for pacifism and pressed for a negotiated peace between equals, all of which led overly zealous critics to take advantage of his background and unjustly charge him with pro-German sentiment. The record does not support these accusations. Villard was strictly, and neutrally, pro-peace for America, for Europe.

Villard claimed credit for Wilson's phrase, "too proud to fight," used in his Philadelphia speech of May 10, 1915. Villard, however, had qualified his original expression with "because there are other and better ways of settling international disputes than by the mass killing of human beings."[61] This phrase is characteristic of Villard's point of view during and after the war, for it emphasized his belief in the dignity of man, his abhorrence of war and his sincere, if idealistic, desire for the "other and better ways of settling international disputes."

When the United States entered the war, Villard, though he had seen it coming, was still deeply shocked, for now he knew that the old isolated America had passed away. "Henceforth we Americans were to be part and parcel of world politics, rivalries, jealousies, and militarism . . . hate, prejudice, and passion were now enthroned in the United States."[62] This he foresaw, and this he fought.

A week after Congress declared war, Villard indicated his stand to his friend and Wilson's aide, Joseph Tumulty. "Believe me," he wrote, "I am ready for any concentration camp, or prison, but I am *not* at war and no one can *put me into war*. . . ."[63] Villard's own war, however, proved far more difficult than most. Against the derision of haughty neighbors, the cool disdain of former companions and the abusive vituperation of misguided patriots, Villard struggled during this war to maintain the liberties familiar to peacetime America. *The Nation* championed freedom of speech in the face of vigorously, frequently overly, enforced sedition laws. It fought conscription of mind as well as body. It attacked the "ferocious sentences" meted out to so-called disloyal persons. It fought to protect the rights of conscientious objectors, even those without church standing, or whose churches failed to prohibit war participation. It rose to the defense of the hounded Socialists, who branded this a capitalist's war. Less than eight months after our entry *The Nation* was declaring "It must be made impossible to plunge this country into war again in the precise way in which it was in April, 1917."[64] Under Villard's leadership it fought the bigotry

---

[60] *Ibid.*, p. 248.
[61] *Ibid.*, p. 257. Villard adds in a footnote, "I have been credited by Ernest Sutherland Bates in his *Story of Congress, 1789-1935*, with being the author of the phrase 'peace without victory' but that is, I believe, an error."
[62] *Ibid.*, p. 324.
[63] *Ibid.*, p. 325. [64] *The Nation*, CV (1917), 711.

and intolerance of a super-patriotic administration with the intense vindicativeness of a persecuted minority, who feeling themselves right, saw the world go mad about them. The Nation's files during these days abound in the sordid records of maliciousness, wickedness and brutality. That things were occasionally otherwise is scarcely noted. The day before the Armistice, T. R. Powell asked the editor, "Is the world really so black as *The Nation* paints it?"

I know that Mr. Burleson isn't perfect, that Mr. Creel is a bit unreliable, that Mr. Gompers isn't Mr. Henderson, that Senator Lodge is unenlightened, that Mr. Roosevelt lacks the judicial temper, that security leagues and councils of safety are often blatant and myopic, that Republicans are protectionists and protectionists not always unselfish, that Negroes are discriminated against on account of race, color, and previous condition of servitude, that judges impose excessive sentences, that conscientious objectors are subjected to indignities, that personal liberty is annoyingly curtailed, that war provokes passion, and I think with the *Nation* that it would be better if it were otherwise. But after all is it so bad as you make it out? What are the objections to amiability and a sense of proportion?[65]

Viewing America at war through pacifist eyes led to darkness and despair; from such depths *The Nation* looked to a peace of brightness and hope and brotherly love as the only salvation of civilized man.

As early as 1916 *The Nation* spoke in favor of a league of nations and refuted the isolationists who declared that such a move would involve us in an entangling alliance. Such a league for peace would not in the least violate the injunction attributed to Washington. "It would not be an alliance at all; and if it were would be disentangling, rather than entangling. It would get us and the rest of the world out of the horrible coil of war."[66] But the primary requirement of any peaceful, stable order was disarmament. "If disarmament does not come, the millions who have died in this war will have died in vain."[67]

In January of 1918, Oswald Garrison Villard released through *The Nation* his fourfold peace and reconstruction program. His "First and foremost" point was universal disarmament, the abolition of conscription and all naval forces. Second, came free trade and freedom of the seas. Third came self-government or government by consent of the governed. This included referenda in transferred or disputed territories. Lastly:

The establishment of an international parliament and an international court, to which latter shall be submitted all issues between nations, dropping once for all the phrase about causes which affect the honor of a nation, precisely as courts between individuals are not in the least affected by the individual honor as such of those who come before it.[68]

[65] *Ibid.*, CVII (1918), 625.
[67] *Ibid.*, CV (1917), 386.
[66] *Ibid.*, CII (1916), 583.
[68] *Ibid.*, CVI (1918), 8.

On the basis of this program *The Nation* took its stand on future international developments. When Wilson presented his "fourteen points" it heartily endorsed them, "For those principles are, in the main, the principles for which the *Nation* has stood, year in and year out, and with increasing ardor of conviction during the war."[69] With the final German collapse *The Nation* set its hopes for the peace treaty.

If it is to be a Junker peace, if the essential, underlying principles of the President's fourteen peace terms are not to be accepted, the world will go on in the same old, stupid way—headed, as Mr. Asquith has just said, for destruction.[70]

Shortly thereafter Mr. Wilson and Mr. Villard sailed for Paris; neither returned the same.

The Nation had advocated a league of nations as its last point in a program which emphasized disarmament and free trade—pacifist liberalism. What came out from Versailles was vastly different, and the disillusioned *Nation* grew ruthless in its attack on "This alliance of victorious Governments, masquerading under the pretentious lying title of a league of nations, organized for sheer economic exploitation. . . ." It spoke of "The Madness at Versailles" and called the league "A Colossal Humbug." Its "liberal" criticism was bitter.

Open diplomacy; freedom of the seas; freedom of trade; disarmament; the principle of self-determination; and the rights of small nations—such was Mr. Wilson's lofty bid for the liberal's toleration of the war. . . . What we have gotten is a connivance hatched in impenetrable secrecy . . . which enables the carrying out of every execrable secret bargain laid down by the Allied Governments since the war began.

What we have is a calm, arrogant, and ruthless formulation of a plan of world-domination by the five conquering powers, a device for causing the exploitable territories of the earth to stand and deliver without the risk and cost of war. . . . The Governments of the United States, Great Britain, France, Italy, and Japan are the league of nations; they are the executive council; they appoint the dummy directors; they pass finally on the qualifications of candidates; they are, in short, an absolute and irresponsible oligarchy. So far from recognizing freedom of the seas, freedom of trade, disarmament, or self-determination, their collusion precluded these possibilities. International commerce cannot be carried on except at their pleasure, under their jurisdiction, and, it is surely by this time superfluous to add, to their profit. Teleologically considered, we are offered an economic alliance which has as its primary object, in general, the exploitation of a propertyless dependent class the world over, and, as between nations, the exploitation of the vanquished by the victors, and of weaker nations by the stronger. . . . It contemplates only a political peace, and that a *pax Romana*. Of economic peace it gives no hint; on the contrary, it contemplates the inauguration of unprecedented economic war.

[69] *Ibid.*, p. 54.
[70] *Ibid.*, p. 502.

This, then, is the ground of objection to the covenant upon which we choose to stand.[71]

Thus *The Nation*, in the name of internationalism and liberalism, fought the League of Nations shoulder to shoulder with the forces of reactionary nationalism. Admitting that the failure of the treaty in the Senate was caused by the nationalists rather than the liberals, *The Nation* still rejoiced in its rejection. For now, with a free hand the United States could prove to the world "That 'American isolation' means no abandonment of international cooperation, no avoidance of international obligations, and no engrossment in selfish or provincial aims."[72]

In the spring of 1920 *The Nation* wrote of the Treaty of Versailles:

We rejoice that the good name of the United States is not to be marred by approval of a document conceived in iniquity and born of imperialistic sin; that the Senate of the United States has refused to approve a document which on its face convicted us of a breach of national faith which was solemnly pledged when Mr. Wilson secured the armistice by the definite promise of peace upon the basis of the Fourteen Points.[73]

Having aided in the defeat of the Treaty of Versailles, and the refusal of the United States to join the League of Nations, *The Nation* had rejected the only positive official program for peace. When at last the United States brought the war to an official end by the joint resolution of Congress, *The Nation* wrote, "We have learned the lesson anew that war accomplishes nothing lasting, settles nothing and destroys infinitely."[74] *The Nation* would have nothing less than pacifist liberalism.

On its sixtieth anniversary, in 1925, *The Nation*, reviewing its record, reaffirmed its earlier stricture against the "madness of Versailles." "The editors would like to believe that if *The Nation* had done nothing else in this decade it would yet have justified itself by the position it then took and has maintained ever since."[75] And still five years later, with the League at the height of its prestige, *The Nation* opposed our entry, for the League "is still part and parcel of that body of death, the Treaty of Versailles, which still prevents the final pacification of Europe. . . ."[76]

With the rejection of the League of Nations, American liberal thought became fractionalized into pacifists, outlawists, and militant internationalists, unable to agree on any positive program. James T. Shotwell has observed that:

The failure to accept the League drove a wedge into liberal opinion and split the peace movement into small groups of bitter, partisan sectaries, too

[71] *Ibid.*, CVIII (1919), 416-417.
[72] *Ibid.*, CIX, (1919), 652.
[73] *Ibid.*, CX (1920), 388.
[74] *Ibid.*, CXIII (1921), 34.
[75] *Ibid.*, CXXI (1925), 6.
[76] *Ibid.*, CXXX (1930), 60.

busily engaged in warring among themselves to do anything effective for peace itself.[77]

The full price for this self-righteous idealism was not felt till some years later.

Beyond its own program of disarmament, free trade, the judicial settlement of international disputes and a peace between equals rather than victors and vanquished, *The Nation* gave fairly dependable support to S. O. Levinson's movement to outlaw war. Though Villard and Levinson did not always agree on details, basically the two programs led in the same direction. Levinson, a Chicago lawyer, thought that in taking recourse to war modern man was utilizing a primitive institution to settle disputes, and by rationally redesigning his institutions he might banish war forever from the world. "He was," noted Quincy Wright, "shocked to discover during World War I that war was legal under international law." By destroying its legality he hoped to rid war of its effectiveness and thus abolish war itself.

His aim was to delegalize it and he thought this could be done by incorporating in international law the principles that the initiation of war is illegal and that the initiator of war should be determined by a world court, should not acquire legal title to the fruits of his aggression, and should not be treated by third states equally with his victim acting in self-defense.[78]

Thus in Levinson's thought were the seeds of the Locarno Treaty, the Kellogg-Briand Pact, and the Stimson non-recognition doctrine.

Levinson's first and most important article outlining his plan appeared in *The New Republic*, March 9, 1918, entitled "The Legal Status of War." Here it was that he described his program to codify international law, to create international courts which would settle all disputes between nations, and to outlaw war as an institution. "In our scheme," Levinson wrote later, "the word war becomes obsolete as an institution. . . ."[79]

The scheme to outlaw war was not original with Levinson. Charles Sumner had anticipated the outlawry of war in his address of 1845 entitled "The True Grandeur of Nations." "If nations can agree in solemn provisions of International Law to establish War as Arbiter of Justice, they can also agree to abolish this arbitrament, and to establish peaceful substitutes," Sumner declared at this time. In the place of war Sumner looked to "A system of Arbitration . . . or a Congress of Nations, charged with the high duty of organizing an *Ultimate*

---

[77] James T. Shotwell, *War as an Instrument of National Policy* (New York: Harcourt, Brace and Company, 1929), pp. 103-104.
[78] John E. Stoner, *S. O. Levinson and the Pact of Paris* (Chicago: The University of Chicago Press, 1942), p. x.
[79] *Ibid.*, p. 195.

Tribunal, instead of 'these battles.' "[80] It was not, however, until Levinson had worked out his own plan that he discovered Sumner.[81]

The program for the outlawry of war was taken up and propagandized by Dr. Charles Clayton Morrison, editor of the *Christian Century,* Senator Borah, John Dewey, James T. Shotwell, and a host of others, while *The Nation* and *The New Republic* gave it a fair amount of space and support. John Dewey, in a *New Republic* article of 1923 wrote that

an inter-national court based on carefully codified law that makes war a crime, having as full jurisdiction in cases of honor as in other cases, is the sole practicable road to the goal which every day is seen the more clearly to be one with the preservation of civilization itself.[82]

But as a first step toward achieving this goal, the entry of the United States into the World Court, the liberals split wide open, with Levinson and his followers standing opposed, *The Nation* and its disciples standing in favor.

In 1920 *The Nation* considered the recently proposed World Court and registered approval, describing it as the "half-loaf" that was better than none. While it was a great advance over the Hague Tribunal, *The Nation* felt that for it to be fully effective a five-point program would have to be adopted.

First, the distinction between justiciable and non-justiciable disputes must be wiped out; second, the court must have power to intervene, and to intervene at all times—the proposed court is to sit only during part of the year; third, there must be immediate international disarmament as the most vital step forward toward safeguarding the court and the peace of the world; fourth, the careful codification of international law must be begun by a group of jurists in international conference; and, finally and most important, there must be an outlawry of war itself.

Following Levinson, *The Nation* declared that outlawry of war "is entirely as practical as was the outlawing of the duel," and, following Villard, *The Nation* added, "and like disarmament it could probably have been obtained at Paris but for the flinching of one man—Woodrow Wilson."[83]

On February 15, 1922, *The Nation* took its stand in favor of the United States' joining the Permanent Court of International Justice, because, for all its defects, it was still free from political control by the League. However, in 1923, in answer to a request by Levinson that *The Nation* change this stand, Villard wrote back, "I am not going to change our policy on the Court, and do not intend to push it, as I con-

[80] Charles Sumner, *Works* (Boston: Lee and Shepard, 1875), I, 51.
[81] Stoner, *op. cit.,* p. 30.
[82] John Dewey, *Characters and Events* (New York: Henry Holt and Company, 1929), II, 669-670.
[83] *The Nation,* CXI (1920), 341.

sider the issue a dead one."[84] Thus *The Nation* drifted on, putting in a good word here for the Court, a bad one there for the League, but always pressing for outlawry, disarmament, and free trade.

The Locarno Pact of 1925 was hailed as "the most hopeful event since that worst of days, August 1, 1914." "If Germany and France can outlaw war with the cooperation of England, Italy, and Belgium," *The Nation* asked, "why not the whole civilized world?"[85] But *The Nation* greeted the Kellogg-Briand Pact with caution and distrust. It was truly a step toward peace, but the various reservations and interpretations deprived it of nearly all genuine effectiveness. However, "If the statesmen who preached peace at the birth of these pacts carry on with the logical consequence of their own words, and begin a real disarming, the world will be reassured."[86] Disarmament was the true path to peace. As a sincere step in that direction *The Nation* recommended that the United States propose to the Geneva Disarmament Conference of 1932 the abolition of the battleship.

> Such a proposal, indicating that we were prepared to make a genuine reduction, would make it possible to secure the international abolition of all aggressive weapons, on land, on sea, and in the air, and thus achieve the beginning of success.[87]

The political scene after World War I was not prepared for the type of liberalism *The Nation* advocated. True to its former policies *The Nation* condemned American imperialism in Haiti, Santo Domingo, Nicaragua, Samoa, and the Philippines, while America went heedlessly ahead with imperialism.

> *The Nation* does not attack American imperialism in the Caribbean or the Pacific primarily in the interest of the people there oppressed or exploited, although that would be a worthy purpose. More important is the effect of such action at home. Imperialism is ingrowing.[88]

It sought democracy, self-government throughout the world—India, Ireland, China, and Russia—and met, it felt, with some success. It fought Mussolini and Fascism when many were agreeing with the New York *Herald Tribune's* comment that "our own legislators have left some people asking whether a Mussolini would not be a valuable addition to Capitol Hill."[89] By 1926, *The Nation* spoke of Italy as "A Nation Gone Mad," while some other critics were thinking only of railroad time-tables.

> It is Mussolini who has become the mad dog of Europe; and those Americans like our bankers who think that we must approve this sort of government of Italy, who pat the dictator on the back and say that it is the duty

---

[84] Stoner, *op. cit.*, p. 106.
[85] *The Nation*, CXXI (1925), 478.
[86] *Ibid.*, CXXXVII (1928), 214.
[87] *Ibid.*, CXXXV (1932), 5.
[88] *Ibid.*, CXIV (1922), 415.
[89] *Ibid.*, CXIX (1924), 5.

POLITICAL LIBERALISM OF NEW YORK *NATION* 91

of liberalism to let Italy have the kind of government it wants, must realize that if this sort of thing goes on the peace of Europe will be in jeopardy as it never was jeopardized by the stupid fumbler of Potsdam.[90]

Yet to oppose this, all *The Nation* could recommend was an agitated international public opinion, "that we shall make felt the weight of our moral indignation against not only what is happening in the Tyrol, but against the Mussolini menace to all Europe."[91]

The Nation watched with dread the progress of Hitler in Germany in the early post-war years. When, in the winter of 1932, Hindenburg invited Hitler into the Cabinet, *The Nation* warned the Germans, "Whatever the difficulties of the situation, there should be no compromise with Hitler." Its estimate of the man was only too accurate. "His becoming the Chancellor could only be a catastrophe for democratic Germany."[92]

Though *The Nation* had no sympathy with dictatorships, it viewed with considerable tolerance the Russian Revolution and its Soviet aftermath. "All hail, free Russia," it wrote upon the occasion of the Russian Revolution of 1917. When, a year later, the Allies entered Russia to put down Bolshevism, *The Nation* loudly protested, for here was a question of self-determination and the sacred right of revolution. Though it did not condone the use of force to achieve reform, nevertheless, it felt that revolution constituted a legitimate exception. On the tenth anniversary of the Revolution *The Nation* dedicated its issue to this "land of hope." Once again *The Nation* made clear that it did not subscribe to communism or approve dictatorial brutality, "but in this muddy age its ten years shine."[93] Out of Russia had come a new ferment in politics which must eventually revitalize the West. In 1929, Villard toured Russia along with other American correspondents, and his judgment fairly reveals the attitude of *The Nation*. For the amazing advances made in industry, agriculture, health and education Villard bestowed the utmost praise; for the violence done to personal liberties he was no less critical.

The Bolsheviks, with all their desire for peace, justice, liberty, and equality for a nation of workers, offer, side by side with tremendous benefits, the methods of a Caesar, a Cromwell, a Franz Joseph, a Nicholas, and a Mussolini.

For using violence and terrorism as a method, the Soviet rulers could not hold the respect of enlightened people. "They can not, I believe, have the sympathy of liberals the world over as long as they pursue this policy," Villard wrote. The argument of the apologists that the end justified the means was "the language of despots from time immemorial. . . . For myself I can see no compromise on this question, no

[90] *Ibid.*, CXXII (1926), 171. [91] *Ibid.*
[92] *Ibid.*, CXXXV (1932), 516. [93] *Ibid.*, CXXV (1927), 495.

argument which shatters the intensity of my belief that those who take the sword shall perish by the sword."[94]

By 1932 the world was well on the course that was to lead to economic dislocation, dictatorship instead of democracy, brutality instead of brotherly love, war instead of peace. In 1923 as *The Nation* watched Mussolini in Italy and "Hitler and his Fascist legionaries in Bavaria" it issued a warning against dictatorships and called for the united opposition of liberals. Its words of that time were equally applicable some years later:

The problem of the hour is to save the slow gains that were made in the period from the French Revolution to the World War. . . . The days when we can afford to sneer at nineteenth-century liberalism are over. If the united front of all the active liberals in the world can but save that liberalism as a starting-point for the future, it is more than we can expect at this moment; it would be enough to carry the hope of our civilization through one of its darkest and most desperate crises.[95]

The union of liberals which *The Nation* envisaged was a union on its terms; peace, disarmament, free trade. Point by point, *The Nation's* hopes were shattered. As the "little Americans" had not availed against the rising tide of imperialism, so now, disillusioned and embittered, the pacifist liberals found their counsel ignored and their program swept aside in the flood of nationalistic reaction and dictatorial militarism.

[94] *Ibid.*, CXXIX (1929), 714.
[95] *Ibid.*, CXVII (1923), 426.

CHAPTER VI

THE TRIUMPH OF BUSINESS POLITICS

The post-Civil War period of reconstruction had come as a challenge to *The Nation's* liberalism. Political corruption and economic chicanery had engulfed President Grant and scandals and swindles reached a shocking total as the Republican party ruled with uncontested supremacy. *The Nation* then challenged the ways of post-war reaction with a plea that the country return to the old liberalism and a separation of politics and economics.

The post-World War I period of reaction offered a striking parallel to the reconstruction years following the Civil War. However, instead of challenging reaction with the old liberals' plea for a separation of politics and economics, *The Nation* countered with the new progressivism. The old *laissez faire* was in disrepute among leftists and rightists. Only as an epithet was it still encountered. A union of politics and economics had come about by the end of the war, and the only remaining question was whether the economy would be controlled from the left or from the right. The pioneer, independent and self-sufficient, had given way to the new American, a service-performing member of the interdependent society. With this transition had come an alteration in the old restraints and the old incentives. Even Elihu Root observed that:

Democracy turns again to government to furnish by law the protection which the individual can no longer secure through his freedom of contract and to compel the vast multitude on whose cooperation all of us are dependent to do their necessary part in the life of the community.[1]

The progressives retained the philosophic basis of the old liberalism but discarded its economic program. The progressive pragmatic approach was, in reality, but a return to the Utilitarianism of Jeremy Bentham. John Dewey, a pragmatist and a progressive, pointed out the new uses of Benthamism:

Utilitarianism, which began its career with the *laissez faire* tendencies of the older liberalism, became, in the hands of the new radicalism, an instrument for appealing to the agencies of organized society in behalf of the common good.[2]

The Nation's post-war change to progressivism was inspired by its new editor, Oswald Garrison Villard. For Villard himself it was a

[1] Elihu Root, *Addresses on Citizenship and Government* (Cambridge: Harvard University Press, 1916), p. 539.
[2] John Dewey, *Characters and Events* (New York: Henry Holt and Company, 1929), II, 838.

change in view brought about by the war and its immediate aftermath. "Anyone with a brain must have moved during those years to the Left or to the Right," Villard later recounted, "and I had gone moderately to the Left." To Villard, basically, the issue was whether one was "for or against the existing political order." He adopted no fixed formula or creed, rejecting both communism and socialism, but looked forward to a greater control of business by the government, and the nationalization of basic industries. "In short, by 1919 I think that I had been emancipated from any merely smug liberalism and social blindness due to the ease and luxury of my upbringing."[3]

The Nation, like a number of other liberals, was inspired by the reorganization of the British Labor Party in 1918 and looked to a similar regeneration in American politics. It was most unlikely that the Republicans or Democrats would adopt the progressive program, and farmer and labor parties had failed miserably in the past,

But if there might now arise, even while the war is going on, a united labor party of industrial workers, intellectual workers, and farmers, the vast body of American sentiment which earnestly desires a better political and economic life than that which we are now living would unquestionably have found a programme and a voice.[4]

To this desire for a new society, a new order, and a new party *The Nation* remained basically faithful. "The old order was political, military, exploitative; the new is economic, industrial, productive."[5] In the face of reaction elsewhere, *The Nation* could well advertise itself now as "the foremost exponent of uncompromising liberalism in America."[6]

Youth is not content, and rightly not content, with shaping its life to conventional ends alone—to marry, "settle down," mow the lawn, drive its own Ford, read the popular magazines, join a lodge, go to the movies, drink grapejuice, vote blatherskites into office, listen to incompetent preachers holding forth on doctrines in which no one with an ounce of grey matter any longer believes, send its children to schools and colleges to have their minds devastated with bad philosophy and worse economics, and get its only excitement occasionally out of the vicarious thrill which accompanies Babe Ruth's feat of knocking a home run.[7]

So, in 1921, wrote Harold Stearns on behalf of the young intellectuals who were now turning to Montparnasse, Berlin, Greenwich Village, and points east to escape from the morass of Main Street. Political-economic dissent in the twenties fell into desuetude as middle-class protest became

[3] Oswald Garrison Villard, *Fighting Years* (New York: Harcourt, Brace and Company, 1939), pp. 461-462.
[4] *The Nation*, CVII (1918), 284.
[5] *Ibid.*, CIX (1919), 390.
[6] *Ibid.*, p. 536.
[7] Harold Stearns, *America and the Young Intellectual* (New York: George H. Doran Company, 1921), pp. 161-162.

enervated by prosperity. The intellectual critics generally by-passed politics and economics in their approach to a higher criticism which would strike at the genteel tradition in literature and the arts, the manners and morals of America, indeed of society itself. *The Modern Temper*, as explained by Joseph Wood Krutch, showed little regard for political economy. Lippmann's *Preface to Politics* of the Progressive period was superseded by his *Preface to Morals* of 1929.

Though the intellectuals sought a new heaven and a new earth, their endeavors served to emphasize the schism in American thought. For, while the intellects thumbed their noses at convention, the majority of Americans became more and more convention-conscious. "To marry, 'settle down,' mow the lawn, drive its own Ford, read the popular magazines, go to the movies, drink grapejuice, vote blatherskites into political office"—these conventional ends were, by and large, the dreams of middle class America. And to realize these goals they quite naturally turned to the political-economic system which they felt would serve this interest. Material prosperity was by tradition the by-product of business endeavor. To achieve and secure prosperity it thus was good politics as well as good economics to implement, promote, and protect business at every turn. Because there was a general absence of restrictive legislation placed upon business during this period, because such restrictive legislation as existed was little enforced, the Republican program has frequently been condemned as a return to *laissez faire*. In truth, however, this was hardly *laissez faire*; it was closer to a modified form of mercantilism, the policy of Alexander Hamilton. The business of government was to foster business.

When the man from Marion, Ohio, was nominated for the Presidency by the Republican party, *The Nation* dubbed him a "Marionette." "In truth," it declared, "he is a dummy, an animated automaton, a marionette that moves when the strings are pulled."[8] But to the country at large such a trait was not without its advantages if business pulled the strings. That this would be the case Harding made clear in his campaign. "We want a period in America," he said, "with less government in business and more business in government."[9] No longer was the *laissez faire* system of vigorous and ruthless competition applauded, for in its place now was a new system of cooperation, association, and consolidation, and the new symbol was service. "Service is the supreme commitment of life," Harding announced in his inaugural address. "I would rejoice to acclaim the era of the golden rule, and crown it with the autocracy of service."[10]

While Harding and the Republicans worked toward the service state in which government would serve business and business serve the people,

[8] *The Nation*, CX (1920), 842a.
[9] Cited in Edward C. Kirkland, *A History of American Economic Life* (New York: F. S. Crofts and Co., 1946), p. 682.
[10] Cited in *The Nation*, CXII (1921), 389.

The Nation, The New Republic, and other liberals sought some explanation for the tragedy that had befallen American liberalism. To *The New Republic* the decline of liberalism in the United States was due "to the unreality which liberals have allowed to pervade liberalism." To *The Nation* such an explanation was impossible. Returning to the anti-war theme, *The Nation* passed its judgment:

> American liberalism is deservedly in eclipse today because it, too, went into the war. For war and liberalism to lie down together anywhere, at any time, with any excuse, means only one thing—disaster to liberalism. When war is declared on a foreign foe it is also declared on every forward-looking cause, every liberal, every reformer at home.[11]

One thing was apparent to all, however; liberalism was in suspension, in fact, in limbo.

Writing shortly before the Harding scandals broke in 1923, the Secretary of Commerce said that "invisible government has greatly diminished."[12] To a large extent this was true because what had formerly been invisible by necessity was now considered to be legitimate, and officially sanctioned. The union of government and business was no longer illicit; their relationships need no longer be conducted surreptitiously. No longer was *laissez faire* the essential component of American individualism. *Laissez faire*, Herbert Hoover noted a decade after Harding's death, "may thrive as an economic or social philosophy in some country today, but it has been dead in America for generations—except in books of economic history."[13] American individualism had found a new basis in the concept of service. But the type of individualism which business sought to promote through the service concept proved, to many Americans, to be more rugged than real. Liberals, also interested in achieving the service state, sought a more direct approach in the form of extended welfare legislation as a means of implementing individualism. Such an approach, however, ran counter to the times. "Under the present conditions in Washington and conditions which have existed ever since I came to Congress," Senator George W. Norris said at the end of his second term, "it is almost impossible to obtain effective legislation in the interest of the people." With a touch of bitterness he added, "I have been bucking this game for twenty years and there is no way of beating it. Now I'm through."[14] In the 1920's there was no more direct route to the people than the channels of business.

[11] *Ibid.*, CXI (1920), 489.
[12] Herbert Hoover, *American Individualism* (New York: Doubleday, Page & Company, 1923), p. 58.
[13] Herbert Hoover, *The Challenge to Liberty* (New York: Charles Scribner's Sons, 1934), p. 51.
[14] Richard L. Neuberger and Stephen B. Kahn, *Integrity, The Life of George W. Norris* (New York: The Vanguard Press, 1937), p. 152. Norris was not through; he continued to serve two more terms.

When Harding died, in 1923, *The Nation* wrote tolerantly, "A genial, kindly, well-meaning, lovable man, typical of a large group of Americans—this was President Harding." But toward his successor to the Presidency it was wrathful:

We doubt if ever before it has fallen into the hands of a man so cold, so narrow, so reactionary, so uninspiring, and so unenlightened, or one who has done less to earn it, than Calvin Coolidge.[15]

Harding at least had had the virtue of a large, if overgenerous, heart; indeed, it was Harding who had pardoned Debs, and this meant much to *The Nation*. On the other hand, all Coolidge could claim was some favorable publicity following an already expired Boston Police strike.

We believe it fitting that Mr. Coolidge should lead the Republican Party in 1924 because it is more than ever before the creature of the big-business interests, of which he is so happy a servant.[16]

Within five months of his taking the oath of office as President, Coolidge gave the key to the politics of his administration. "The business of America is business," he told the American Society of Newspaper Editors.[17] This was no *laissez faire* program in which the government would stand by as a neutral policeman. On the contrary, this was dollar diplomacy abroad and dollar persuasion at home. In his inaugural address of 1925 Coolidge survey the happy scene and portrayed in glowing words the interventionist theory of government.

Here stands our country, an example of tranquility at home, a patron of tranquility abroad. Here stands its government, aware of its might but obedient to its conscience. Here it will continue to stand, seeking peace and prosperity, solicitous for the welfare of the wage-earner, promoting enterprise, developing waterways and natural resources, attentive to the intuitive counsel of womanhood, encouraging education, desiring the advancement of religion, supporting the cause of justice and honor among the nations.[18]

If the promotion of enterprise in the ensuing years appeared more tangible than the solicitousness for the wage-earner, it was only because, according to the service concept, the juices of prosperity would have to seep down from above. Thus, the fruits of prosperity would have to be squeezed first by business.

"Coolidge was business, big business, little business, the magnified horsetrade which is American commerce," William Allen White has written.[19] With Andrew Mellon, "the greatest Secretary of the Treasury since Alexander Hamilton," Herbert Hoover, promoter of trade

[15] *The Nation*, CXVII (1923), 152.
[16] *Ibid.*, CXVIII (1924), 696.
[17] William Allen White, *A Puritan in Babylon* (New York: The Macmillan Company, 1938), p. 253.
[18] *Ibid.*, p. 315.
[19] *Ibid.*, p. 377.

associations as Secretary of Commerce, and William Howard Taft as Chief Justice of the Supreme Court, the ways of business were secure. Even appointments to the bench were checked to make sure they stood in line. "Thus the financial and commercial world and the political world in the days of the Coolidge bull market grew in beauty side by side in the creation of a federal judiciary."[20] In all branches of government the forces of business economy were in triumphant control. What resulted was not *laissez faire* but business politics, or intervention from the right and for the right. No longer was the issue one of intervention or non-intervention as it had been in the post-Civil War period; now the only argument was whether government should be by business and for business or by the public and for the consumer. And during the 1920's there was little point in argument.

In those days when the snail was on the thorn and God was in his Heaven business men crowded into the White House until the luncheon guest-list looked sometimes like a chart of interlocking directorates of high finance.[21]

A comparison of the policies of President Coolidge and the United States Chamber of Commerce reveals an almost exact parallel. Both favored a reduction in corporation and individual income taxes, the abolition of excise taxes and the inheritance tax; both favored subsidies to business, such as the merchant marine subsidy; both looked askance at anti-trust legislation; both endorsed the Department of Commerce foreign commerce service; both opposed the McNary-Haugen Bill. "In the booming stock market," William Allen White concludes, "the President and the United States Chamber of Commerce were making one big noise in the same rain-barrel."[22]

The political-economic theory of this period was nowhere clearly and succinctly summed up. It must be gathered from the random phrases that truly expressed the politics of business plutocracy as it was actually practiced in subsidy, promotion and non-restraint. Perhaps the nearest approach to a spokesman of this theory may be found in William E. Humphrey, influential member of the Federal Trade Commission. Writing in *The Magazine of Wall Street* on April 5, 1927, Humphrey revealed the new attitude of post-war politics as it affected the executive, legislative and judicial branches of government, as well as the independent regulatory commissions. "The President instead of scoffing at big business, does not hesitate to say that he proposes to protect the American investor wherever he may rightfully be." This was in accordance with the wishes of the legislative branch. "Instead of passing obstructive laws for political purposes, Congress now satisfies its demagogic tendencies by ordering all sorts of investigations—which come to nothing." The courts in turn had pretty well emasculated the anti-trust

---

[20] *Ibid.*, p. 348.
[21] *Ibid.*, p. 335.
[22] *Ibid.*, pp. 396-397.

laws. "It is not that the courts flout statutory law, but that they interpret it in harmony with economic law. They are changing with the people and the times." The Courts simply followed the example of the Secretary of Commerce.

The Secretary of Commerce, far from appealing to Congress for legislation regulatory of business, allies himself with the great trade associations and the powerful corporations—not to benefit them as such but to benefit the people through them. . . .

The independent regulatory commissions, as the appointed keepers of the business conscience, in turn had fallen into line.

The Federal Trade Commission has completely reversed its attitude toward the business world. . . . The Interstate Commerce Commission has become the bulwark instead of the oppressor of the railways.

In truth there had come about in America a "wholesale fusion of political and economic life."[23]

This was not *laissez faire*. It was surely not democracy, for democracy was at a low ebb.[24] Rather was it plutocracy, the service state in which government served business so that benefits might seep down to the people. Writing in 1926, William Allen White observed, "What a sordid decade is passing! It will be known in American history fifty years hence as the time of terrible reaction. . . ."[25]

"It is certainly curious that so outspoken a journal as *The Nation* should have survived for 60 years," George Bernard Shaw wrote its editor in 1925, "in a country where Truth is tarred and feathered, lynched, imprisoned, clubbed, and expatriated as undesirable three times a week or so."[26] But *The Nation* and its seemingly lost causes carried on. Not the least of its causes was its effort to establish and promote an effective, progressive third party in middle class American politics. In 1920 it announced a progressive platform which emphasized free

[23] Cited in part in Harvey Wish, *Contemporary America* (New York: Harper & Brothers Publishers, 1945), p. 370. S. E. Morison and H. S. Commager, *The Growth of the American Republic* (New York: Oxford University Press, 1937), II, 534-536. William Allen White, *A Puritan in Babylon*, p. 334.

[24] Some idea of the degradation of the democratic dogma during this period may be had by reference to the United States Army *Training Manual*, No. 2000-25 (Government Printing Office, 1928), p. 91. Here democracy is defined as "a government of the masses. Authority derived through mass meeting or any other forms of 'direct' expression. Results in mobocracy. Attitude toward property is communistic—negating property rights. Attitude toward law is that the will of the majority shall regulate, whether it be based upon deliberation or governed by passion, prejudice, and impulse, without restraint or regard to consequences. Results in demagogism, license, agitation, discontent, anarchy." Cited in Merle Curti, *The Growth of American Thought* (New York: Harper & Brothers Publishers, 1943), p. 696.

[25] William Allen White, *The Autobiography of William Allen White* (New York: The Macmillan Company, 1946), p. 632.

[26] *The Nation*, CXXI (1925), 7.

trade, free speech, free press and free assembly, the reduction of military expenses, and a speedy and just peace with Germany. "The thought of the country is unquestionably turning strongly in the direction of Federal ownership or control of transportation, mines, forests, water power, and other natural resources or monopolies. . . ."[27] As between the Republican and Democratic candidates in 1920 *The Nation* refused to choose. "There is no choice between them."[28] That left Eugene Debs, still in Atlanta penitentiary, and Christensen as the only candidates in the field. "The vote of protest is never a vote lost," *The Nation* advised its readers.

If it is the vote of conscience, it ennobles; if it is the genuine expression of the voter it uplifts the ballot, and throwing it away on a man and a party for whom the voter has no respect besmirches it.[29]

By 1922 *The Nation* was calling upon liberals to revolt from the major parties and establish a new one. "The old parties are but creatures of a worn-out and rotten economic system," it declared. "There is no hope from them. And yet the country is astir, waiting the signal for revolt." Such a signal, *The Nation* hoped, would come from one of the recognized liberal political leaders, and it looked hopefully toward an anti-war isolationist. "In this situation a great responsibility rests upon Senator Borah, to whom Liberals and Radicals and even many conservatives are turning as to a savior."[30] Borah, however, preferred to be a Republican. Later that year, *The Nation* jubilantly announced the birth of the third party with the alliance of the Farmer-Labor party and the Nonpartisan League.

This farmer-labor alliance, with its name a witness of its economic basis, is, we believe, the most hopeful political movement since the birth of the Republican Party in anti-slavery days. . . . It is far and away the best thing that has happened to America since the war welded upon us the political and economic despotism from which, as this election shows, we *are* emerging.[31]

By 1924 *The Nation* was calling upon La Follette, and successfully, to head the third party. Here, now was the hope of a reformation in politics, that "regrouping into conservatives and progressives which the country needs if we are to be capable of thinking along politico-economic lines. . . ."[32]

The Conference for Progressive Political Action was heartily supported by *The Nation*. Oswald Garrison Villard took a personal part in the La Follette campaign, touring the country with Vice-Presidential Candidate Wheeler and serving as Assistant National Treasurer of the Progressives. The Progressive platform was basically *The Nation's*

[27] *Ibid.*, CX (1920), 164.
[29] *Ibid.*, p. 314.
[31] *Ibid.*, p. 541.
[28] *Ibid.*, CXI (1920), 32.
[30] *Ibid.*, CXV (1922), 140.
[32] *Ibid.*, CXIX (1924), 88.

program. Opposition to monopoly, reaffirmation of civil rights, public ownership of public power and transportation systems, retention of high taxes on high incomes, reconstruction of the Federal Reserve system to provide greater public credit control, guarantee to workers of the right to organize and bargain collectively, creation of a government marketing corporation to protect the farmer and consumer alike, protection to cooperatives, ratification of the child labor amendment, abolition of injunctions in labor disputes, opposition to imperialism and dollar diplomacy—all these had appeared in *The Nation* before they were adopted by the Conference for Progressive Political Action. The only new items to appear were the Congressional over-riding of Supreme Court decisions and the election of federal judges for limited terms, and these *The Nation* now endorsed.[33] For a while it seemed as though the British Labor Party had found its counterpart in America. The Conference for Progressive Political Action

represented the first formal alliance of organized labor in America with farmers and Socialists. The American Federation of Labor, departing momentarily from its traditional policy of non-partisan political action endorsed the candidacies of La Follette and Wheeler.[34]

But the movement never quite took hold. "It is a story repeated often in American politics," one of its supporters later wrote, "a certain amount of liberal sentiment with nowhere to go."[35] *The Nation*, however, refused to despair.

We do not—we cannot lose heart; we can only see the need for greater and greater efforts, for persistent, continued, and devoted patriotic service to the end that all the people shall see where lies salvation and where is the high road to American ideals.[36]

Of La Follette, *The Nation* wrote at the time of his death, "he was closer to the people and closer to the soil of America than almost any other great politician since Lincoln."[37]

In 1925 *The Nation* issued "A Progressive Platform," which it hoped the Progressives would adopt at their Chicago convention as "an entering wedge for the bringing back of the government to the people." Because it discloses *The Nation's* concept of progressivism it is of value to quote it at length.

[33] It is interesting to note that at the time *The Nation* sought to curtail the power of the courts within the United States, it sought to extend unlimited jurisdiction to an international court, where even issues of policy and national honor would be settled by juridical process.

[34] Kenneth Campbell MacKay, *The Progressive Movement of 1924* (New York: Columbia University Press, 1947), p. 9.

[35] Norman Hapgood, *The Changing Years* (New York: Farrar & Rinehart, 1930), p. 280.

[36] *The Nation*, CXIX (1924), 510.

[37] *Ibid.*, CXXI (1925), 4.

1. Direct nomination and election of the President; a national referendum, especially on war. Revision of the Constitution to place the Cabinet on the floor of Congress for a regular question-hour; to provide for the immediate installation of a newly elected Congress; to abolish the electoral college and to make nation-wide referenda possible;

2. Government ownership of natural resources, such as water-power, super-power, and mines. The development and operation of the remaining water-power to be by the government;

3. Government ownership of railroads and pipelines;

4. Free trade, and immediate liberalization of the present immigration laws;

5. Ratification of the child-labor amendment to the Constitution;

6. Equal rights for all women;

7. Indorsement of consumers' and producers' cooperation; existing obstacles thereto to be removed;

8. Abolition of the injunction in labor cases; labor's right to bargain collectively and to organize free from the danger of persecution under anti-trust and other laws;

9. Foreign policy: The outlawry of war; complete disarmament; the flag not to follow the investor; our forces to be withdrawn from the Caribbean republics; elimination of oil and business concessions as the directing force in our foreign policy; reduction of foreign debts to us in return for concessions as to disarmament and economic reconstruction abroad; a genuine big-brother attitude toward American republics in place of the present bloody, militaristic policy;

10. Economy, honesty, and efficiency in government, introduced by men pledged to govern in the interest of the whole people and not in the name of the great interests;

11. Free press, free speech, and restoration of the personal liberty guaranteed by the Constitution but now subject to hourly violation by officials of the government from police officers up; summary punishment of officials who fail to uphold the Constitution in these respects.[38]

Absent in this program is anything akin to the McNary-Haugen bill to benefit the farmers. "The farmers' salvation lies chiefly in cooperation, in the abolition of the tariff, and in the opening up of foreign markets" plus a government-sponsored marketing corporation.[39] *The Nation* was opposed to subsidy and protection.[40]

As the election of 1928 approached, *The Nation* renewed its plea for "a new and clean peoples' party."

If there was reason to demand a new party in 1920 there are many more reasons today, for during the years that have elapsed the great forces of intrenched capital have been marching on, gaining in vigor and strength and

[38] *Ibid.*, CXX (1925), 175.
[39] *Ibid.*
[40] During the next few years its stand on the McNary-Haugen bill wavered slightly, so that by 1927 it tolerated it; yet in 1928 it approved Coolidge's veto of it.

in their control of the resources which rightfully belong to the whole people.[41]

However, it soon became evident that a choice would have to be made among Hoover, Smith, and Norman Thomas. Hoover was automatically out as far as *The Nation* was concerned, thus the choice narrowed down to Smith (" a candidate of whom the great capitalists are not in the least afraid") and Thomas (a "high-grade," "honorable candidate").[42] Under such circumstances it would have been entirely natural for *The Nation* to stump for Norman Thomas, a member of its editorial staff. Smith had only a "trend to progressiveness" while Thomas, "In personality and platform . . . comes closest to the principles for which *The Nation* stands."[43] Yet *The Nation* failed to give Thomas an exclusive endorsement. Perhaps this was due to the wave of bigotry and religious intolerance that swept into American politics around the name of Al Smith—at any rate, *The Nation* found him a "symbol of tolerance in American life" and threw the choice between Smith and Thomas open to its readers, while still calling for a new third party itself. "To our readers we can again only appeal not to cast their ballots for Herbert Hoover, but to choose between Smith and Thomas, as their consciences shall dictate."[44]

The Nation's failure to give a clear and undivided endorsement of Norman Thomas in 1928, and its continued insistence upon organizing still a new third party was a great disappointment to the Socialists. Harry W. Laidler wrote to the editor after the election of 1928 enquiring,

in view of the changing attitude of the country, and in view of the fact that there is no other, coherent progressive group on the horizon at the present time, should not *The Nation* use its influence to encourage, rather than discourage, genuine progressives to support the Socialist Party during the coming months?[45]

The Nation's position on this, however, was surprisingly realistic.

We regret that we cannot join Mr. Thomas in believing that we should build up the Socialist Party, but we cannot forget that for most Americans socialism connotes only bolshevism or anarchy. Hence a new designation and a revised program upon which all liberals may unite are the demand of the hour.[46]

The Republican victory brought forth the familiar call from *The Nation:* "Now is the time to plan for a union of forces to create a

[41] *The Nation,* CXXVI (1928), 709.
[42] *Ibid.,* CXXVII (1928), 30, 31.
[43] *Ibid.,* p. 284.
[44] *Ibid.,* p. 440. *The Nation's* poll of its subscribers announced November 7, 1928, revealed the following alignment: Smith—6,872, Thomas—2,830, Hoover—2,784, Foster—431, Will Rogers—27.
[45] *Ibid.,* p. 660.
[46] *Ibid.,* p. 536.

truly liberal party which shall take for its own the best of the issues discarded by the Democrats during their gradual moral disintegration."[47] For the main strength of such a party it looked to the ranks of the Democrats, where there was still a wide marginal fringe of liberalism.

We wonder if within the Democratic Party itself there are not a lot of able and clean men ... who are ready to strike out for a new deal, who realize that a rebirth of the Democracy into a great fighting instrument for liberalism at home and abroad is an impossibility.[48]

In 1927, the twentieth-century de Tocqueville, André Siegfried, visited the United States and, from his observations, produced the popular commentary, *America Comes of Age*. Like his predecessor, he was skeptical of the spiritual virtues of American democracy while greatly impressed, for all its cultural stereotypes, with its material achievements. "It is a materialistic society," he noted, "organized to produce things rather than people, with output set up as a god."[49]

Behind this materialism, the emphasis on goods rather than good, were the twin concepts of a business civilization, production and profit. Unconsciously at first, but later deliberately, it became the fixed policy of the government to foster both. And, by and large, the American people had faith in this new "American system." Writing on "Business the Civilizer" Earnest Calkins explained the new theory in the *Atlantic Monthly* in 1928, when he wrote that "the work that religion, government, and war have failed in must be done by business.... That eternal job of administering this planet must be turned over to the despised business man."[50] The business man, however, was hardly despised, indeed he had become ennobled. He had become the man whom everybody knew and respected, the beneficent servant of society.

The new business service concept of government made accepted economic and political theory strangely unrealistic, certainly out of date. America was still democracy and practicing something close to *laissez faire*, but, in reality, for the while at least, both of these had passed away.[51] Political scientists discovered and condemned highly organized and highly financed pressure groups and lobbyists, but their grapplings with the more outward manifestations of the new era would not down the pervasive problems of business-sponsored publicity, legislation, and

---

[47] *Ibid.*, p. 510.
[48] *Ibid.*, p. 536.
[49] André Siegfried, *America Comes of Age* (H. H. Hemming and Doris Hemming, Translators), (New York: Harcourt, Brace and Company, 1927), p. 348.
[50] Earnest Elmo Calkins, "Business the Civilizer," *Atlantic Monthly*, CXLI (February, 1928), 157.
[51] "So little has *laissez faire* worked under actual experience that all the powers of the government have actually had to be invoked to preserve a certain amount of compulsory 'free competition.'" Walter Lippmann, *A Preface to Morals* (New York: The Macmillan Company, 1929), p. 244.

administrative and judicial control.[52] Economists and political scientists still talked in terms of bifurcated authority, economic and political, the twentieth-century equivalent of the medieval doctrine of the two swords. Now business at least attempted the union of the political and economic sovereigns, for the while releasing man from the trying obligation of serving two masters.

A Lehman Brothers banker, Paul M. Mazur, expressed a not uncommon conviction of the new business concept when he wrote of the orthodox economists:

It may well have been that the economic conditions of Europe a century ago, or more, were determined or at least modified by the economic theses of Smith, Ricardo or Mill. But in America the forces of business have moved too fast for the building of an effective industrial philosophy upon the theories of even the best informed of our economists.[53]

Mazur then went on to explain the American prosperity of 1928 in terms of the triumph of the business men. "Modern economic conditions and even principles are the results of the thoughts and actions of business men."[54] He was willing to bestow a certain amount of credit upon the government.

That the present administration in Washington has been helpful cannot be denied. Calvin Coolidge has impressed upon the American business man many a conception of Federal government that has been highly encouraging to American industry. . . . Mr. Coolidge and his administration have undeniably contributed to the kind of confidence that makes for good business. . . .[55]

With business and government working cooperatively toward the same objectives, the future of American prosperity seemed secure indeed. "These next ten years are to be a stirring decade in the annals of American business," Mazur wrote in 1928. "While industry dominates the thought of America, there need be no fears—a cataclysm aside—for the future of American business."[56]

It was this faith in the combined business and government-sponsored prosperity which swept Hoover into the Presidency in 1928. *The Nation* and its reformer fringe stood outside the main current of American thought. Lincoln Steffens, writing of the Republican victory observed, "It was all business. In brief, that was an economic election

---

[52] "To a very considerable degree the writer on politics to-day is about where the economist was when all economic theory began and for all practical purposes seemed to end with Robinson Crusoe and his man Friday. Nobody takes political science very seriously, for nobody is convinced that it is a science or that it has any important bearing on politics." *Ibid.*, p. 260.
[53] Paul M. Mazur, *American Prosperity* (New York: The Viking Press, 1928), p. vi.
[54] *Ibid.*
[55] *Ibid.*, p. 76.
[56] *Ibid.*, pp. 262, 267.

which sent to the White House Herbert Hoover to do what he is trying to do: to represent business openly, as Coolidge and other presidents had covertly."[57]

Herbert Hoover brought to America the clearest, most conspicuous example of the service concept of government and business cooperation. It was the Hamiltonian dream made real. In 1929, Hoover spoke approvingly of how "Hamilton's vision well comprehended the necessities of Federal Government activity in support of commerce and industry."[58] Addressing the Gridiron Club in April of 1929, he explained the idea of the advancement of service through government cooperation.

Our form of government can succeed only by cooperation—not only by cooperation within the administrative arm of the Government and cooperation with Congress, but also by cooperation with the Press, cooperation with business, and the cooperation in social leadership.[59]

Presumably, if farmer, labor or more radical elements were to be admitted to this happy circle they would be included under "social leadership."

" 'Service' is a combination of the civic virtue of the Protestant, the materialism of Bentham, and devotion to progress," André Siegfried had observed in 1927. "In the end, 'service' is the doctrine of an optimistic Pharisee trying to reconcile success with justice."[60] For a while, however, it served its purpose in America. Perhaps no finer tribute to its temporary validity could be found than *True Story Magazine's* report, in 1930, of the type of material that was submitted for publication. "From tales of misery and privation and struggle ten years ago," *True Story* noted, "the stories that now pour in to us from all quarters of America are tales of ultimate success and happiness."[61]

Success and happiness were the keynotes of the conservatism of America during the prosperous twenties, even though the prosperity did not always succeed in seeping down to farmers and workers. The spirit of prosperity gave added impetus to the trend toward conservatism which made the American temper of the late 1920's vastly different from that of 1912. Thus, the historian, Samuel Eliot Morison, noted in 1929 that:

The United States has evolved from a country of political experiment, a debtor to Europe, a radical disturber of established government, the hope of the oppressed and an inspiration to all men everywhere who wished to be

[57] Lincoln Steffens, *The Autobiography of Lincoln Steffens* (New York: Harcourt, Brace and Company, 1931), p. 857.
[58] William Starr Myers (ed.), *The State Papers and Other Public Writings of Herbert Hoover* (New York: Doubleday, Doran & Company, Inc., 1934), I, 69.
[59] *Ibid.*, I, 30.
[60] Siegfried, *op. cit.*, p. 179.
[61] *The American Economic Evolution* (New York: *True Story Magazine*, 1930), p. 8.

free; into a wealthy and conservative country, the world's banker and stabilizer, the most powerful enemy to change and revolution.[62]

When the crash came *The Nation* was as much surprised as its most vigorous opponents. A brief recession perchance, it felt, but no calamity. "The great task of the next few months is the restoration of confidence," *The Nation* announced conservatively,

> Confidence in the fundamental strength of the financial structure notwithstanding the strain that has been put upon it, confidence in the essential soundness of legitimate industry and trade.

Rather than take advantage of the collapse, it quietly observed that "Criticism of Wall Street will not help much. . . ."[63]

As Hoover summoned business leaders from all over the country to White House conferences at which cooperative stabilization plans to check unemployment were mapped out, *The Nation* exclaimed, "Economics is king in Washington. Who shall rule the king?"[64] President Hoover, addressing the Conference of Business Leaders at the Chamber of Commerce quite properly noted that, "This is a far cry from the arbitrary and dog-eat-dog attitude of the business world of some thirty or forty years ago."[65]

It was this conference of government officials and industrial and financial leaders which struck Lincoln Steffens as being

> an historical event of some significance. It was a recognition, however informal and unaware, of the truth Stinnes had seen in Germany, Mussolini in Italy, and the Bolsheviki in Russia, that the government of business and the political government should be one.[66]

> The Harding way was the old, the politician's way. The Coolidge way was the new American, the old English, the respectable, businesslike way of representing business, and that Hoover personified. No need of bribing him, no excuse for any graft in the White House. Bribery and corruption were over. President Hoover, like Coolidge, honestly believed that the government should favor big business, without price. And so, when the economic crisis came, President Hoover could call together the big business men to counsel and agree with him on a business political policy which he and they should join in carrying out. All in the open. . . . The engineer president was bringing to the throne, formally and publicly, the potential heads of our two actual governments: the industrial government and the political government. . . . A victory. A Marriage. One can't sneer any more that Washington is the kept woman of Wall Street. They are man and wife, and that changes everything; it makes the old wrong right. It makes Washington a decent woman.[67]

[62] Cited in Preston William Slosson, *The Great Crusade and After, 1914-1928* (New York: The Macmillan Company, 1930), p. v.
[63] *The Nation*, CXXIX (1929), 614.
[64] *Ibid.*, CXXX (1930), 142.
[65] William Starr Myers, *op. cit.*, I, 183.
[66] Lincoln Steffens, *The Autobiography of Lincoln Steffens*, p. 856.
[67] *Ibid.*, pp. 863-864.

The combined efforts of business and government, however, acting within the framework of the cooperative service philosophy, proved unable to stop the depression, for the so-called causes of prosperity no longer caused prosperity. The time was ready for a new deal, a new approach.

The Nation came to oppose the Hoover administration at nearly every turn. It found it "bankrupt—intellectually, morally, and politically." It called its handling of the depression "Government by Abstention." The Smoot-Hawley tariff was "a crime against the American people—yes, against the whole world." *The Nation*, believing the government ought to be "an agency of public service" stood for Muscle Shoals, which Hoover opposed. *The Nation* despaired of the existing economic system which Hoover relied on, a system based on "higgledy-piggledy private effort guided only by prices in the mad rush for profits." "What we need," *The Nation* wrote in the fall of 1930, "is, bold, comprehensive economic planning.... We must coordinate our productive forces so as to produce regularly the things we need and to distribute them to the people who need them."[68] *The Nation* sought a broad program of unemployment relief and unemployment insurance and attacked the President's failure to move vigorously in this direction.

In the matter of unemployment and unemployment relief Mr. Hoover is at his most shining empty best. There must be no government aid for the jobless. "I am opposed to any direct or indirect government dole," he said. Large business and financial corporations may be assisted by federal loans or other means, but the man out of work must not look to Washington for help.[69]

While *The Nation* favored expenditure of large sums of money for relief, direct government assistance, yet it opposed the pump-priming endeavors of the Reconstruction Finance Corporation. It feared that such an attempt to maintain price levels would, in fact, prolong the depression. Indeed, its criticism in the depths of the depression of 1932, sounded much like the old-time conservative. "Successful or not, no government has a right to engage in such a gamble.... What will happen if that gamble fails?"[70]

By 1932, it seemed to middle-class progressives that mere temporizing expedients would fail and that a more radical reform was required. "We are facing a new era," Louis Adamic wrote in January of that year. "This is a time of transition and profound frustration, of agony and decay."[71] While in June, 1932, Reinhold Niebuhr wrote that "the

[68] *The Nation*, CXXXI (1930), 434.
[69] *Ibid.*, CXXXIII (1931), 656. Stuart Chase used the R.F.C. in much the same way in his *A New Deal*, published in August before the election. "If there is a banker or a business man decrying the heresy of that two billions of collectivism known as the Reconstruction Corporation, I have not heard his voice." Stuart Chase, *A New Deal* (New York: The Macmillan Company, 1932), p. 61.
[70] *Ibid.*, CXXXV (1932), 156.
[71] Louis Adamic, "The Collapse of Organized Labor," *Harper's Magazine*, CLXIV (January, 1932), 178.

middle-class paradise which we built on this continent, and which reached its zenith no later than 1929, will be in decay before the half-century mark is rounded."[72] No wonder that later that year Calvin Coolidge declined all offers for any further public office. "We are in a new era to which I do not belong," Coolidge said, "and it would not be possible for me to adjust myself to it."[73]

As the election approached *The Nation* advertised "It is better to waste a vote on Thomas than on Hoover or Roosevelt."[74] Oswald Garrison Villard wrote a series of articles for *The Nation* entitled "The Pot and the Kettle" in which he attacked the two major parties. "The man who votes for either Hoover or Roosevelt is the one who is throwing away his vote," Villard explained. "He is again turning the country over to the bosses, or their owners, the great capitalists." The only hope for the country lay in a large protest vote for Norman Thomas. Such a heavy vote "will make both the old parties sit up and take notice, and encourage those who desire a third liberal party without the Socialist name."[75] Along with Villard in the Thomas camp in 1932 were such progressives as Morris L. Ernst, Morris R. Cohen, Reinhold Niebuhr, Elmer Davis, John Dewey, and Lewis Gannett. Shortly before the election, on October 31, 1932, Herbert Hoover declared in a campaign speech at Madison Square Garden: "This campaign is more than a contest between two men. It is more than a contest between two parties. It is a contest between two philosophies of government."[76] Still, as between Hoover and Roosevelt, the Republicans and the Democrats, *The Nation* saw no real choice.

The Nation's uncanny sense for lost causes prevailed again, and for the fourth successive presidential election it endorsed the loser. Grateful for the Hoover defeat, although greatly disappointed in the Thomas vote, it wrote that the election gave some cause for encouragement,

Even though the change to a Democratic Administration offers no worthwhile program, and none of the far-reaching changes so desperately needed to extricate us from the disaster in which the country finds itself. . . .[77]

The Nation had sustained the enfeebled progressive movement from 1918 to 1932, the progressive movement that was not to come into power until the New Deal. However, although many progressives saw in the election of Franklin Roosevelt the triumph of progressivism, *The Nation* saw in this victory simply a continuation of the time-worn scheme of things. That the New Deal gave promise of some re-alignment in

[72] Reinhold Niebuhr, "Catastrophe or Social Control?" *Harper's Magazine*, CLXV (June, 1932), 118.
[73] William Allen White, *A Puritan in Babylon*, p. 439.
[74] *The Nation*, CXXXV (1932), ii, facing p. 221.
[75] *Ibid.*, p. 299.
[76] William Starr Myers, *op. cit.*, II, 408.
[77] *The Nation*, CXXXV (1932), 470.

American politics into liberal and conservative groupings, that the dynamic Roosevelt would lead the movement toward a new freedom by greater government intervention in the economic sphere and greater responsibility of business to government, that a gigantic public power project would be inaugurated in the Tennessee Valley, that labor and agriculture would be boosted as never before, that reciprocal trade agreements and the Good Neighbor policy would be put into effect—that, in short, most of the various progressive political-economic programs which *The Nation* had sponsored from 1918-1932 would be inaugurated under the coming administration, *The Nation* failed to anticipate.

CHAPTER VII

THE PROGRESSIVE COURSE OF LIBERALISM

"The protest against authoritarian rule in successive areas—religion, politics, social relations, economic affairs—defines the progressive course of Liberalism."[1] Liberalism, to be a truly significant political movement, must keep ever on the move, responding in creed to the progressive changes in social institutions and organizations. It must be, in Woodrow Wilson's striking analogy, like the Red Queen who had to run very, very fast, if she wanted to keep in the same place. The freedoms of the past have a way of making possible the servitudes of the present. As social institutions transform themselves they present new problems in authority and restraint, and the zealous liberal finds that the struggle must take on new forms and new foes in order to preserve the liberties that now exist. It was the realization that the struggle for liberty was a continuing one and not one already achieved that separated the progressivism of Villard from the liberalism of Godkin.

Having succeeded in achieving religious and political liberty, liberals, not unnaturally, thought of the Union victory in the American Civil War as the final and culminating triumph of liberalism. Democratic enlightenment, seemingly, had been victorious against oligarchic privilege, and the way now seemed clear for free men all over America to live freely together in the good society. With a static conception of social institutions, the old liberals seemed to believe that the claims of liberalism were now exhausted by their victory, and man's long sad saga of oppression and restraint had ended in the glorious freedom of 1865.

Though the seeds of the old liberalism lay buried deep in antiquity, its modern manifestation budded in the late eighteenth century. Mid-nineteenth-century England and America saw its fairest bloom. In its eighteenth-century form liberalism had sought to remove such artificial restraints as prevented the individual from attaining his full stature in his religious, political and economic life. But, though the age of reason brought to man a sense of dignity, a belief in progress and a faith in the efficacy of rational effort—all of which became basic to the liberal tradition, it imposed upon man the static conceptions of the times. It was a mechanistic age, an age of force relationships in which observable causes had discernible effects. It was a Deistic age in which an intelligible and benevolent Deity maintained an orderly and harmonious universe. It was the age of rationalism in which man beheld the natural order and found that, with but a few minor alterations, it might be very

[1] Jacob H. Hollander, *Economic Liberalism* (New York: The Abingdon Press, 1925), p. 13.

good. All science, art, government, and economics were reducible by reason to basic laws and formulae. Thus, the generation that developed a mechanistic conception of government discovered the same principles in economics. Checks and balances had their economic counterpart in supply and demand. In such an age one might be forgiven for positing a world of laws instead of men. Old chaos vanished from man's ken and in its place appeared the cosmos. Now was the latter day triumph of Sir Isaac Newton, of whom Alexander Pope had written:

> Nature and Nature's laws lay hid in Night:
> God said, *Let* Newton *be*! and all was Light.[2]

Mankind need only apply these natural laws to social, political and economic institutions. By rooting out the unnatural, the unnecessary and the arbitrary, man would achieve his greatest freedom in accordance with natural law. Eighteenth-century liberals thus saw in autocratic mercantilistic government and a hereditary class society the great foes of freedom. Political freedom required democracy; economic freedom, *laissez faire*; and social freedom, equality. These then became the tenets of late eighteenth-century liberalism and the United States of America its proving ground.

As liberalism developed it presented itself as a combination of two separate, though converging strains of thought. The natural rights philosophy of Jefferson and Paine joined with the utilitarianism of Smith, Bentham, and Mill to seek a social system in which the individual might grow and develop with the least amount of external control and direction. Such a system was not only natural, but from the utilitarian point of view, its consequences were socially desirable. Thus in the newly created American commonwealth, the liberal ideal appeared to be realized, with the exception of slavery which Lowell called "the single disturbing element."[3] America was to the youthful Godkin and his liberal friends the "promised land." "To the scoffs of the Tories that our schemes were impracticable, our answer was that in America, barring slavery, they were actually at work."[4] Now, in 1865, the shackles of slavery were removed as had been the shackles of autocratic government in 1776. Surely, the fulfillment of the liberal dream was at hand. The great liberal battles were over; all that now remained

---

[2] Alexander Pope, *The Complete Poetical Works of Alexander Pope* (Cambridge Edition; Boston: Houghton, Mifflin Company, 1903), p. 135. A more current reaction may be had in Hilaire Belloc's rejoinder:
> It did not last: the Devil howling "HO!
> Let Einstein be! restored the status quo."
Cited in *Oxford Dictionary of Quotations* (London: Oxford University Press, 1941), p. 26.

[3] James Russell Lowell, *Works* (Boston: Houghton, Mifflin and Company, 1888), V, 217.

[4] Rollo Ogden (ed.), *Life and Letters of Edwin Lawrence Godkin* (New York: The Macmillan Company, 1907), I, 11-12.

were the necessary mopping-up campaigns: the purification of government, the eradication of the spoils system, and a hastened return to *laissez faire*.

In the meantime, however, the economic system in America was undergoing a radical change. Built upon a natural rights conception of property and a utilitarian conception of individualism, it was passing beyond the bounds of both. The free enterprise system was founded upon the principle of the social responsibility of the individual. So firmly entrenched was this belief that the sole proprietor was subject under the laws of liability to the severest penalties for acts, or failures to act, which led to socially undesirable consequences. Both employer and employee assumed before the law the fullest measure of responsibility. In economic life, this marked the pinnacle of individualism. But the age of reason brought forth the basic inventions which were to revolutionize the system of production. The social system built upon the economics of exchange now had to accommodate itself to the economics of production. The new technique by which large aggregations of wealth could be brought together to finance the modern system of mass production was found in the post-Civil War development of the corporate form of business organization. The rise of the modern corporation effected the decline of the old individualism. The corporation supplanted individual effort with social effort and in so doing, eliminated the severities of full personal liability. In the modern corporation are the beginnings of socialization in our economic life. Formerly, the individual strove alone and bore the full burden of his responsibilities. Under the corporate form of business enterprise, however, he worked in concert with other stockholders, and his responsibilities were curtailed by the laws of limited liability. The success of this new form of economic organization may be seen in its astounding growth in the United States in the years following the Civil War. Equally astounding is the ease with which liberalism revised its basic concepts to accommodate the corporate device and its subsequent alterations in our economic life. The right to property passed beyond the simple ownership of land into the intangible area of "business." The corporation was considered a person. That the change in the modes of production and control in our economic life, its emphasis on group effort and delimitation of individual responsibility, had drastically altered the context of individualistic liberal thought *The Nation* and its late nineteenth-century colleagues failed to understand.

Late nineteenth-century liberalism fought for freedom within the context of late eighteenth-century institutions. Accustomed to oppressive government in the past, it saw in government only an instrument for oppression in the future. It mistook legal equality for actual equality. In its eagerness to release mankind from the restraints of autocratic mercantilistic government, it made possible the oppressions as well as the freedoms of the new economic system.

In the post-Civil War period the paths of utilitarianism and the natural rights philosophy diverged. Where, formerly, the two systems of thought had led to the same conclusions, they now led in opposite directions. Natural rights posited the sanctity of individual property rights; utilitarianism, which considered rights only as they contributed to socially desirable consequences, sought to modify the property rights doctrine and went on to include an ever-widening field of activity within the concept of public utility. The old liberalism, built upon the union of natural rights and utilitarianism, now had to reconcile itself to their divergence. *The Nation* chose the conclusions of the former while claiming adherence to the method of the latter. It defended the absoluteness of rights that had been espoused by the utilitarians of an earlier generation. The socio-economic life of America had undergone a revolutionary change in the nineteenth century. *The Nation*, however, clung to the static liberalism of the eighteenth. It decried the natural rights philosophy while accepting its conclusions; it claimed adherence to utilitarianism while rejecting the answers utilitarianism now found. As early as 1867 a *Nation* reviewer took note of the new trend of utilitarianism toward government intervention.

> What . . . has done most to promote the love of "interference" is . . . the steady progress of the utilitarian theory of politics amongst that portion of the population whose opinions most strongly affect legislation—we mean the large reforming class which has within the last thirty years sprung up in all the more highly civilized countries, and which occupies itself actively and incessantly with all questions bearing on the social, moral, and physical condition of the poorer classes. The leaders of this movement, in so far as it has any political bearing, have been utilitarians of the Bentham school, and the most marked feature in their system has been their dislike of all absolute principles in politics.[5]

Where nineteenth-century liberalism failed, it failed because of its reluctance to accept the consequences of its own utilitarianism. Whereas eighteenth-century liberals feared government because it was autocratic, nineteenth-century liberals feared government because it was democratic and capable of incorporating utilitarian judgments into law. In seeking the goal of individual freedom, nineteenth-century liberals denied the method that would make this goal really significant. Natural rights and utilitarianism, so happily joined in the middle of the nineteenth century, had split, and their divergence appeared in the conflict between corporate capitalism and democratic progressivism. "Can it be believed that the democracy which has overthrown the feudal system and vanquished kings, will retreat before tradesmen and capitalists?" de Tocqueville had

[5] *The Nation*, V (1867), 372.

asked.[6] Progressives now sought the democratic answer to this inquiry. In spirit the new progressivism was more a resurgence of liberalism than a separation from it. It reaffirmed the liberal belief in the possibility of progress, the rationality of men, and reason and discussion as the proper methods of effecting ordered changes in society. But where late nineteenth-century liberals had emphasized individual rights as absolute and irrevocable, twentieth-century progressives founded their ethics upon the utilitarianism of Bentham. "It is this social interpretation of rights which characterizes the democracy coming into being," Walter Weyl observed in 1912, "and makes it different in kind from the so-called individualistic democracy of Jefferson and Jackson."[7] Absolute rights liberalism was now met with the progressive concept that "liberty is a function of the social conditions existing at any time."[8] Rights cannot remain static in a changing society but must vary to keep pace with the changes in social institutions. The pioneer concept of the individual who enjoyed rights against society was replaced with the social concept of the individual who lived in society and derived his rights from it. "An individual right, then," wrote L. T. Hobhouse, "cannot conflict with the common good, nor could any right exist apart from the common good."[9] To the progressive, as to Jeremy Bentham, the criterion for judging any action, whether undertaken by the individual or by the state, was its social consequences. The social consequences that determined the desirability of *laissez faire* in Bentham's day, proved to the progressive, now that the economic system had changed, the desirability of strategic state intervention. Writing of the progressives' indebtedness to Jeremy Bentham, John Dewey said,

When he disallowed the doctrine of inalienable individual natural rights, he removed, as far as theory is concerned, the obstacle to positive action by the state whenever it can be shown that the general well-being will be promoted by such action.[10]

Having removed the theoretical restrictions on government intervention in the economic sphere, the progressives were now prepared to use democracy as the instrument for achieving a wide scale application of the dictates of utilitarian ethics.

The control exerted over the individual directly by the government may, as a matter of fact, be slight in comparison with that which is exercised through the various agencies which control the economic system.[11]

[6] Alexis de Tocqueville, *American Institutions* (Boston: John Allyn, 1874), I, 5-6.
[7] Walter E. Weyl, *The New Democracy* (New York: The Macmillan Company, 1912), pp. 161-162.
[8] John Dewey, *Liberalism and Social Action* (New York: G. P. Putnam's Sons, 1935), p. 34.
[9] L. T. Hobhouse, *Liberalism* (New York: Henry Holt and Company, Home University Library edition), p. 127.
[10] Dewey, *op. cit.*, p. 19.
[11] J. Allen Smith, *The Spirit of American Government* (New York: The Macmillan Company, 1912), p. 305.

The task of the progressive now was either to remove those economic controls or else make them more responsible to society. This called for positive government action. "The program of a government of freedom must in these days be positive, not negative merely," Woodrow Wilson wrote of the new freedom.[12] The old liberals, clinging to a static concept of economic rights that took little cognizance of economic changes, believed liberty to exist wherever government regulation was absent. The new progressives, basing their concept of economic rights on current economic conditions, sought positive government assistance to make more meaningful the phrase "equality of opportunity." "We must use political liberty to introduce a greater measure of economic equality, or economic inequality will destroy political liberty."[13] The old liberals were inclined to believe equality of opportunity achieved when slavery was abolished. Thus there developed an apparent conflict between liberty and democracy which took on a rather dramatic form in America with the organization of Liberty Leagues, composed mainly of rich men and Industrial Democrats, for the most part laborites.[14]

Late nineteenth-century liberals were inclined to despair of democracy as it tended to intervene in the economic sphere; twentieth-century progressives saw in such intervention the only hope for democracy's survival. "It is not true that democracy has been tried and found wanting," C. E. M. Joad declared. "What is true is that democracy has been found to be difficult and not tried."[15]

The old liberals, identifying liberalism with capitalism, resisted any governmental alterations of the economic system. The progressives, identifying liberalism with social democracy, sought to modify capitalism in order to extend liberty.

Democracy as we understand it at present, means liberalism applied to the political field. What we now need to learn is how to make it work in the field of economics. . . . Wherever we turn, in other words, we need to learn how to apply liberalism instead of giving it up.[16]

Progressivism was, indeed, a resurgence of the liberal democratic faith.

From 1865 to 1932 the developing pattern of *The Nation's* political editorials and comments reveals the transition in American thought from a formalized liberalism to a flexible progressivism. Within the frame-

---

[12] Woodrow Wilson, *The New Freedom* (New York: Doubleday, Page and Company, 1921), p. 284.
[13] C. E. M. Joad, *Liberty To-Day* (London: Watts & Co., 1934), p. 201.
[14] George Soule, *The Future of Liberty* (New York: The Macmillan Company, 1936), p. 54.
[15] Joad, *op. cit.*, p. 192.
[16] Julius Seelye Bixler, *Conversations with an Unrepentant Liberal* (New Haven: Yale University Press, 1946), p. 11.

work of the old liberalism, the Godkin *Nation* fought the good fight for human freedom, honest government and a pure society. Within the outlines of progressivism, the Villard *Nation* carried on the same struggle.

In the prospectus announcing the purposes of the newly founded *Nation*, the editors declared some of their main objects to be:

The discussion of the topics of the day, and above all, of legal, economical, and constitutional questions, with greater accuracy and moderation than are now to be found in the daily press.

The maintenance and diffusion of true democratic principles in society and government, and the advocacy and illustration of whatever in legislation or in manners seems likely to promote a more equal distribution of the fruits of progress and civilization. . . .

The fixing of public attention upon the political importance of popular education and the dangers which a system like ours runs from the neglect of it in any portion of our territory.[17]

These objectives are, indeed, the liberal's basic articles of faith. Public education is the means by which all men may receive that minimum of training so essential to the making of rational decisions. The faith in public education registers the belief that the common man is capable of learning and that the case for democracy rests upon his fitness. Accurate discussion of public topics expresses the belief that through discussion the truth may be ascertained and that the function of a liberal journal is to present as accurately as possible the basic issues so that a rational decision may be made. The advocacy of whatever legislation appears to promote a more equal distribution of the fruits of progress reasserts the liberal belief that democracy and liberty cannot exist without a firm and underlying core of equality. "The maintenance and diffusion of true democratic principles in society and government" is once again the liberal clarion call of old.

To these basic objectives the prospectus added:

The *Nation* will not be the organ of any party, sect, or body. It will, on the contrary, make an earnest effort to bring to the discussion of political and social questions a really critical spirit, and to wage war upon the vices of violence, exaggeration, and misrepresentation by which so much of the political writing of the day is marred.[18]

The Nation travelled an independent course through these sixty-seven years, and on more than one occasion stood very much alone.

In its early years *The Nation* was basically optimistic. It jubilantly proclaimed the Northern victory as a final triumph of democratic ideals. With slavery abolished, the last vestiges of class distinction and privi-

[17] Cited in *The Nation*, XXXX (1886), 516.
[18] *Ibid.*

lege in America had been destroyed. But in order to strengthen the principle of equality it was necessary that suffrage restrictions be the same for all. Equality meant that each should be limited only by his abilities, not by legal restraints based on race or sex. Each individual, seeking his own selfish interests, limited only by the laws of morality and a minimum of state regulation, would bring to himself a maximum of happiness. And—with an astounding leap in logic—what was true for one was also true for the community.

Not only had democracy emerged triumphant from the Civil War, but with the triumph had come a new historical interpretation of our political system. No longer were the people of the states considered joined together by compact, voluntary or involuntary, but bound organically by common heritage, language, blood, and purpose. The fact of the nation was old, but the concept was new, for it was a recognition of the new socialization in our political ideas. In this new society, rights were not divinely authorized nor brought from a state of nature, but rather arose simply from the dictates of expediency. The only basis for personal rights was their utility. In the economic field it was claimed that the industrial progress of the times was attributable to the free actions of men possessing the rights of property and contract. For such an assumption to prove just and proper, one had to posit a general harmony of interests among men and nations, for only with this hypothesis could one believe that the free actions of individuals within the moral law would necessarily benefit society as a whole. And for the most part, *The Nation* was willing to accept this assumption. The early phase of *The Nation's* thought was marked by an optimistic belief in the essential tenets of liberal democracy and a faith in the future progress of America under democratic government. It had faith in the common sense of the American people, whose judgments, while not infallible, proved generally to be right. While critical in its analysis, it nevertheless, made a point of extolling the virtues of our democratic system.

Within a decade of its founding, however, *The Nation* grew skeptical of its early optimism. Believing in the finality of its own political and economic judgments, it saw a rapidly expanding industrial society burst the seams of its static liberalism. It tried to fit the pattern of the new order upon the framework of the old. It tried to apply *laissez faire* principles to late nineteenth-century America when there were few who cared to listen and fewer still to obey. As it observed unruly democracy running loose, *The Nation* became disillusioned. It lost its enthusiasm for Negro suffrage; it opposed woman's suffrage. It sought every device to check democracy rather than to expand it. It accepted now the corporate form of business as an individual economic unit possessed of the personal rights of individuals; yet it saw in trade unionism only a new form of tyranny. Whereas it had seen previously the desirability of government interferences on behalf of the Negro, it now doubted the value of any form of government interference on behalf of any class. Any assumption of a harmony of interests among individuals was now modified by a reassertion of the Malthusian theory of population expansion and the acceptance of the doctrine of natural selection in the economic order. The demand for free competition became modified accordingly by the belief that competition was actually harmful under certain circumstances, and where it was, combination was not only natural but beneficial.

While *The Nation* accepted the corporate modifications in our economic system and their underlying philosophical implications, it became increasingly severe in its attacks on the developing political system. It advocated civil service reform to check the spoils system and the direct primary and proportional representation to check the power of the bosses. It became fearful of the power of majorities, for it saw in the rising number of poor and ignorant not a malady in our economic system, but only a disturbing danger to democracy. Its faith in the common sense of the mass of the people waned as it looked increasingly to a government by the property-owners and the intelligent members of society. Though it saw no satisfactory alternative to the democratic processes, it now became increasingly aware of the vices of the system, and its articles reveal a dyspeptic pessimism. It attacked the tendency of a democracy to place mediocre men in public office. Majority rule made it possible for the reason of the few to be cast aside by the passion of the mob which threatened violence not only to property and contracts, but further, to the absolute laws of economics.

Ineffective in checking government intervention at home, *The Nation* and the old liberal remnant dedicated their last best effort to resisting late nineteenth-century imperialism. Here was an issue in which natural rights could join with utilitarianism, and liberals from both schools responded in force. But the liberalism that had been victorious in 1865 met defeat in the Spanish-American War, though no doubt its protests were effective in conditioning the judgment of later Americans against imperialism as a national policy.

Under the guise of morality the Godkin *Nation* attempted to preserve a modified version of the shop-keeper's theory of economics in late nineteenth-century industrial America. It attempted to impress the people with the necessity of virtue in an age of corruption and political sculduggery. It sought to bring reason and intelligence into the affairs of men in a period when passions and emotions ran high. However, because it attempted to preserve an individualistic interpretation of utilitarianism in an age when the philosophy of Bentham had been adapted to the needs of social legislation, it fell into a vigorous defense of the late nineteenth-century economic *status quo* and thus became the backbone of American conservatism. Though it always pressed for respectable reforms, it resisted every political-economic change that was truly significant. It failed to see that trade unionism was the disguised form of the corporate device, which maximized collective effort and minimized individual responsibility. It failed to see that government, to be effective, must possess a jurisdiction at least as great as the corporations or groups which are subject to its authority. It failed to see that liberty is not necessarily enhanced by the absence of governmental restraint, but by the absence of restraint wherever it may occur. It failed to see that liberty, upon examination, always becomes a question of whose liberty to do what? and that, therefore, in a democracy, determinations of liberties always involve the utilitarian criterion of social consequences. It failed to see that where restraint is necessary, the task of the liberal is to make the sources of restraint responsible to society. It was, in all, these deficiencies which made the old liberalism politically obsolete and opened the path to the new progressives and, in fact, the new *Nation*.

The old *Nation* applauded the hanging of the Chicago Anarchists; the new fought for Sacco and Vanzetti. The old denounced Debs; the new, in 1920, urged its readers to vote for him or Christensen. The old *Nation* saw in social legislation a reversion to a medieval world of fixed prices and wages; the new *Nation* saw in it the beginning of a new society.[19]

Thus did I. F. Stone emphasize the difference between *The Nation* of Godkin and that of Villard. Oswald Garrison Villard, who became editor of *The Nation* in 1918, liked to think that, with a few minor changes, he was simply carrying on the Godkin tradition. However, the engrafting of progressivism upon liberalism involved basic changes in policy, for all the underlying similarities in thought. *The Nation* continued as caustic and independent as before; it lambasted greed and corruption in politics wherever it was found. It had no mercy on friend or foe as it continued the holy war for public and private morality. It kept reason and conscience on their eighteenth-century pinnacle. It was, as before, a citizen of the world and met provincialism with an international approach. But the policies of the Villard *Nation* took on a new emphasis that was lacking in *The Nation* of earlier days. Thus, the new *Nation* departed from the old not only on the issue of governmental intervention in the economic sphere but on the issues of pacifism and civil liberties.

Primary to Villard's policies was his belief in pacifism, a belief which decidedly affected *The Nation's* viewpoint from 1918-1932. Godkin had maintained a decided abhorrence of war as a national policy. It was the faith of the old liberals that men were by nature peacefully disposed and could be harmoniously bound together in amicable interdependence by the rational policy of free trade. But they never denied

[19] *Ibid.*, CL (1940), 159.

the necessity of adequate armament for defense or the last-ditch necessity of war for self-preservation. What they objected to was war for aggression and conquest. Villard and the new *Nation* carried the abhorrence of war to the extreme of pacifism and tended to believe that wars did not come to those who did not seek them and that therefore one must only act righteously in international politics to be treated righteously by others. Because the new *Nation* could brook no compromise with its principles of pacifism, it dealt in international affairs with an abstract world of reason instead of men, as had the old *Nation* in political economy. In its effort to achieve all or nothing, it rejected the League of Nations as a compromise with evil and thus threw out the baby with the bath.

Whereas the old *Nation* seldom made an issue of civil liberties, the new *Nation* scoured the country for instances of their denial and gave them full publicity. By and large, after reconstruction, the lynchings of the Negro, the discriminations against labor leaders, the inequalities practiced against women, and the servitudes of the new immigrants, passed unnoticed in the Godkin *Nation*. To Villard, these were flaming issues. A founder of the National Association for the Advancement of Colored People, Villard returned *The Nation* to its original position in regard to the Negro. In their original prospectus in 1865 the editors of *The Nation* had included the cause of the Negro as among their primary objectives. Thus they advocated:

The earnest and persistent consideration of the condition of the laboring class at the South, as a matter of vital interest to the nation at large, with a view to the removal of all artificial distinctions between them and the rest of the population, and the securing to them, as far as education and justice can do it of an equal chance in the race of life.

The enforcement and illustration of the doctrine that the whole community has the strongest interest, both moral, political, and material, in their elevation, and that there can be no real stability for the Republic so long as they are left in ignorance and degradation.[20]

Godkin had started off enthusiastically enough in favor of the Negro, but within a decade his ardor had cooled. Now, under Villard *The Nation* picked up the original theme.

Whereas Godkin had given only lukewarm support to the feminists, and this only during his first few years as editor, Villard developed the woman's rights issue to the magnitude of a major crusade. It was to the new *Nation* the ancient liberal struggle for equality. The new *Nation* flaunted its banner of freedom in the face of Ku Klux Klanism, 100% Americanism, and the super-patriotism of the twenties that found all dissenters subversive. It espoused the freedom of men to speak and write about James Joyce, Soviet Russia and free love, as it defended

[20] Cited in *ibid.*, XXXX (1886), 516.

Henry Ford's right to expound anti-Semitism. It reaffrmed the old faith in truth discerned through free discussion. It fought for the release of conscientious objectors from concentration camps, an executive pardon for Mooney and Billings, and a new trial for Sacco and Vanzetti. Within the framework of progressivism it fought for equality, freedom—social, political and economic—and democracy. Though it seldom won its battles, it nevertheless served to keep alive the tenets of the liberal democratic faith in an age that saw that system on the wane.

In 1932 the change in the editorship of *The Nation* coincided with the election that brought to the United States a basic change in governmental policy. In a sense, this election gave dramatic emphasis to the difference between the old liberalism and the new. Where it served to highlight the new system it did so by reasserting that liberal democracy, to be meaningful, requires as great an adherence to liberalism as it does to democracy itself. Democracy provides the method of liberalism. Liberalism provides the goal of freedom and the faith in man, the philosophical bases of democracy. Liberalism without democracy becomes the empty creed of the late nineteenth-century Manchester school which, losing faith in the common man, in turn despaired of democracy. Such dogmatists were then liberals in name only. Democracy without liberalism soon ceases to be democratic but becomes rather the shibboleth of a system aristocratic in nature and oligarchic in control. Liberalism and democracy must walk hand in hand.

The course of American liberal democratic thought, the union, the separation, and the reunion of liberalism and democracy are nowhere more clearly portrayed than in the successive issues of *The Nation* magazine. "Here, encompassed in the span of one journal's life," its present editor has truly written, "you find the whole story of freedom's struggle to adapt to, and so survive, the inexorable growth of industrial collectivism."[21] With this in mind, no doubt, Raymond Gram Swing said, "I can think of no single periodical in the United States whose continued existence is of more importance to American democracy than *The Nation*."[22]

[21] *Ibid.*, CL (1940), 145.
[22] *Ibid.*, CLI (1940), Back cover, following page 20.

BIBLIOGRAPHY

PRIMARY SOURCE

The Nation (New York), Volumes I-CLI (1865-1940).

SECONDARY SOURCES

BOOKS

Adams, Charles Francis. *An Autobiography: 1835-1915.* Boston: Houghton, Mifflin Company, 1916.
Adams, Henry. *The Education of Henry Adams: An Autobiography.* Boston: Houghton, Mifflin Company, 1918.
American Economic Evolution, The. True Story Magazine, Publishers, 1930.
Bancroft, Frederic. *Speeches, Correspondence and Political Papers of Carl Schurz.* New York: G. P. Putnam's Sons, 1913. 6 volumes.
Bancroft, George. *Miscellanies.* New York: Harper and Brothers, 1855.
Barker, Ernest. *Political Thought: From Herbert Spencer to the Present Day.* Home University Library Edition. New York: Henry Holt and Company.
Beard, Charles A. *An Economic Interpretation of the Constitution of the United States.* New York: The Macmillan Company, 1914.
Bellamy, Edward. *Looking Backward.* New York: The Modern Library.
Bleyer, Willard Grosvenor. *Main Currents in the History of American Journalism.* Boston: Houghton, Mifflin Company, 1927.
Bowen, Catherine Drinker. *Yankee from Olympus.* Boston: Little, Brown and Company, 1944.
Bowen, Francis. *American Political Economy.* New York: Charles Scribner's Sons, 1870.
Bowers, Claude G. *Beveridge and the Progressive Era.* New York: The Literary Guild, 1932.
Brewer, David J. *American Citizenship.* New York: Charles Scribner's Sons, 1902.
Bryce, James. *The American Commonwealth.* Second Edition. London: Macmillan and Co., 1891. 2 volumes.
———. *Studies in Contemporary Biography.* New York: The Macmillan Company, 1903.
Buck, Solon J. *The Agrarian Crusade.* New Haven: Yale University Press, 1920.
———. *The Granger Movement.* Cambridge: The Harvard University Press, 1913.
Carey, Henry C. *Miscellaneous Works.* Philadelphia: Henry Carey Baird, 1875.
Carnegie, Andrew. *Triumphant Democracy.* New York: Charles Scribner's Sons, 1886.
———. *Triumphant Democracy.* Revised Edition. New York: Charles Scribner's Sons, 1893.
Carpenter, W. S. *The Development of American Political Thought.* Princeton: The Princeton University Press, 1930.

Chamberlain, John. *Farewell to Reform: The Rise, Life and Decay of the Progressive Mind in America.* Second Edition. New York: The John Day Company, 1933.

Chase, Stuart. *A New Deal.* New York: The Macmillan Company, 1932.

Coker, Francis W. *Recent Political Thought.* New York: D. Appleton-Century Company, 1934.

Commons, J. R., et al. *History of Labor in the United States.* New York: The Macmillan Company, 1918. Volume II.

Cowley, Malcolm and Smith, Bernard. *Books that Changed Our Minds.* New York: Doubleday, Doran and Company, Inc., 1939.

Croly, Herbert. *The Promise of American Life.* New York: The Macmillan Company, 1911.

Curti, Merle. *The Growth of American Thought.* New York: Harper & Brothers Publishers, 1943.

Dana, Richard H., III (ed.) *Richard Henry Dana, Jr. Speeches in Stirring Times and Letters to a Son.* Boston: Houghton, Mifflin Company, 1910.

Denslow, Van Buren. *Principles of the Economic Philosophy.* New York: Cassell & Company, Limited, 1888.

Dewey, John. *Characters and Events.* New York: Henry Holt and Company, 1929. 2 volumes.

———. *Liberalism and Social Action.* New York: G. P. Putnam's Sons, 1935.

Dorfman, Joseph. *Thorstein Veblen and His America.* New York: The Viking Press, 1934.

Dunning, William A. *Essays on the Civil War and Reconstruction.* New York: The Macmillan Company, 1910.

———. *A History of Political Theories.* New York: The Macmillan Company, 1920. Volume III.

Elliot, Hugh S. R. (ed.). *The Letters of John Stuart Mill.* London: Longmans, Green and Co., 1910. Volume II.

Ely, Richard T. *Ground Under Our Feet.* New York: The Macmillan Company, 1938.

Filler, Louis. *Crusaders for American Liberalism.* New York: Harcourt, Brace and Company, 1939.

Fine, Nathan. *Labor and Farmer Parties in the United States, 1828-1928.* New York: Rand School of Social Science, 1928.

Gabriel, Ralph H. *The Course of American Democratic Thought.* New York: The Ronald Press Company, 1940.

Garrison, W. P., and Garrison, F. J. *William Lloyd Garrison, 1805-1879: The Story of His Life, Told by His Children.* New York: The Century Co., 1889. Volume IV.

Geiger, G. E. *The Philosophy of Henry George.* New York: The Macmillan Company, 1933.

George, Henry. *Progress and Poverty.* New York: The Modern Library.

George, Henry, Jr. *The Life of Henry George.* Toronto: The Poole Publishing Company, 1900.

Godkin, Edwin Lawrence. *Problems of Modern Democracy.* New York: Charles Scribner's Sons, 1903.

———. *Reflections and Comments, 1865-1895*. New York: Charles Scribner's Sons, 1896.
———. *Unforeseen Tendencies of Democracy*. Boston: Houghton, Mifflin and Company, 1898.
Godwin, Parke. *A Biography of William Cullen Bryant*. New York: D. Appleton and Company, 1883.
Greeley, Horace. *The Autobiography of Horace Greeley, or Recollections of a Busy Life*. New York: J. B. Ford & Co., 1872.
———. *Political Economy*. Boston: James R. Osgood and Company, 1871.
Hapgood, Norman. *The Changing Years: Reminiscences of Norman Hapgood*. New York: Farrar & Rinehart, 1930.
Haynes, Fred E. *Social Politics in the United States*. Boston: Houghton, Mifflin Company, 1924.
———. *Third Party Movements Since the Civil War*. Iowa City: The State Historical Society of Iowa, 1916.
Hicks, John D. *The Populist Revolt*. Minneapolis: The University of Minnesota Press, 1931.
Hillquit, Morris. *History of Socialism in the United States*. New York: Funk & Wagnalls Co., 1910. Fifth Edition.
Hoar, George F. *Autobiography of Seventy Years*. New York: Charles Scribner's Sons, 1903. 2 volumes.
Hobhouse, L. T. *Liberalism*. Home University Library Edition. New York: Henry Holt and Company.
Hobson, J. A. *Richard Cobden: The International Man*. London: T. Fisher Unwin, Ltd., 1918.
Hofstadter, Richard. *Social Darwinism in American Thought*. Philadelphia: University of Pennsylvania Press, 1945.
Hollander, Jacob H. *Economic Liberalism*. New York: The Abingdon Press, 1925.
Hoover, Herbert. *American Individualism*. New York: Doubleday, Page & Company, 1923.
———. *The Challenge to Liberty*. New York: Charles Scribner's Sons, 1934.
Jordan, David Starr. *The Blood of the Nation: A Study of the Decay of Races Through the Survival of the Unfit*. Boston: American Unitarian Association, 1906.
Jacobson, J. Mark. *The Development of American Political Thought*. New York: D. Appleton-Century Company, Inc., 1932.
Kelley, William D. *Speeches, Addresses and Letters on Industrial and Financial Questions*. Philadelphia: Henry Carey Baird, 1872.
Kirkland, Edward C. *A History of American Economic Life*. Revised Edition. New York: F. S. Crofts & Co., 1946.
Lecky, William Edward. *Democracy and Liberty*. New York: Longmans, Green and Co., 1896. 2 volumes.
Lerner, Max. *Ideas Are Weapons*. New York: The Viking Press, 1939.
Lewis, Edward R. *A History of American Political Thought*. New York: The Macmillan Company, 1937.
Lippincott, Benjamin Evans. *Victorian Critics of Democracy*. Minneapolis: The University of Minnesota Press, 1938.

Lippmann, Walter. *Drift and Mastery: An Attempt to Diagnose the Current Unrest.* New York: Mitchell Kennerley, 1914.
———. *A Preface to Morals.* New York: The Macmillan Company, 1929.
———. *A Preface to Politics.* New York: Mitchell Kennerley, 1914.
Lloyd, Henry Demarest. *Wealth Against Commonwealth.* New York: Harper & Brothers Publishers, 1894.
Lowell, James Russell. *Works.* Boston: Houghton, Mifflin and Company. Volume V, 1888; Volume VI, 1894.
MacKay, Kenneth Campbell. *The Progressive Movement of 1924.* New York: Columbia University Press, 1947.
Mahan, Captain A. T. *The Interest of America in Sea Power, Present and Future.* Boston: Little, Brown and Company, 1917.
Maine, Sir Henry Sumner. *Popular Government.* London: John Murray, 1885.
Marcet, Mrs. Jane H. *Conversations on Political Economy.* Philadelphia: Moses Thomas, 1817.
Martyn, Carlos. *Wendell Phillips: The Agitator.* New York: Funk & Wagnalls, 1890.
Mazur, Paul M. *American Prosperity: Its Causes and Consequences.* New York: The Viking Press, 1928.
Merriam, C. Edward. *A History of American Political Theories.* New York: The Macmillan Company, 1903.
———. *American Political Ideas.* New York: The Macmillan Company, 1926.
Mill, John Stuart. *Autobiography of John Stuart Mill.* New York: Columbia University Press, 1924.
Moon, Parker Thomas. *Imperialism and World Politics.* New York: The Macmillan Company, 1936.
Morgan, Arthur E. *Edward Bellamy.* New York: Columbia University Press, 1944.
Morison, Samuel Eliot, and Commager, Henry Steele. *The Growth of the American Republic.* New York: Oxford University Press, 1937. Volume II.
Mott, Frank Luther. *American Journalism: A History of Newspapers in the United States through 250 Years, 1690 to 1940.* New York: The Macmillan Company, 1941.
Myers, William Starr (ed.). *The State Papers and Other Public Writings of Herbert Hoover.* New York: Doubleday, Doran & Company, Inc., 1934. 2 volumes.
Neuberger, Richard L., and Kahn, Stephen B. *Integrity: The Life of George W. Norris.* New York: The Vanguard Press, 1937.
Nevins, Allan (ed.). *Letters of Grover Cleveland.* Boston: Houghton, Mifflin Company, 1933.
———. *The Evening Post.* New York: Boni and Liveright, 1922.
Nineteenth Century, The: A Review of Progress. New York: G. P. Putnam's Sons, 1901.
Noblin, Stuart. George William Curtis and Edwin Lawrence Godkin as Reform Leaders in the United States, 1865-1900. Unpublished master's thesis. Department of History, University of North Carolina, Chapel Hill, North Carolina, 1935.

Norton, Charles Eliot. *Letters of Charles Eliot Norton.* Boston: Houghton, Mifflin Company, 1913. 2 volumes.
—— (ed.). *Letters of James Russell Lowell.* New York: Harper & Brothers, 1894. 2 volumes.
—— (ed.). *Orations and Addresses of George William Curtis.* New York: Harper & Brothers, 1894. 3 volumes.
Ogden, Rollo (ed.). *Life and Letters of Edwin Lawrence Godkin.* New York: The Macmillan Company, 1907. 2 volumes.
Oxford Dictionary of Quotations. Oxford University Press. London, 1941.
Parrington, Vernon Louis. *Main Currents in American Thought.* New York: Harcourt, Brace and Company, 1930.
Payne, George Henry. *History of Journalism in the United States.* New York: D. Appleton and Company, 1920.
Phillips, Wendell. *Speeches, Lectures, and Letters.* Boston: Lee and Shepard, 1884.
Perry, Arthur Latham. *Principles of Political Economy.* New York: Charles Scribner's Sons, 1891.
Pope, Alexander. *The Complete Poetical Works of Alexander Pope.* Cambridge Edition. Boston: Houghton, Mifflin Company, 1903.
Powderly, Terence V. *The Path I Trod.* Edited by Harry J. Carman and others. New York: Columbia University Press, 1940.
Pringle, Henry F. *Theodore Roosevelt.* New York: Harcourt, Brace and Company, 1931.
Raymond, Daniel. *The Elements of Political Economy.* Baltimore: F. Lucas and E. J. Coale, 1823. 2 volumes.
Riley, Woodbridge. *American Thought from Puritanism to Pragmatism.* New York: Henry Holt and Company, 1915.
Root, Elihu. *Addresses on Citizenship and Government.* Cambridge: Harvard University Press, 1916.
Schlesinger, Arthur M., Jr. *The Age of Jackson.* Boston: Little, Brown and Company, 1945.
Schurz, Carl. *The Reminiscences of Carl Schurz.* New York: The McClure Company, 1908. 3 volumes.
Shotwell, James T. *War as an Instrument of National Policy and Its Renunciation in the Pact of Paris.* New York: Harcourt, Brace and Company, 1929.
Siegfried, André. *America Comes of Age.* Translated by H. H. Hemming and Doris Hemming. New York: Harcourt, Brace and Company, 1927.
Slosson, Preston William. *The Great Crusade and After, 1914-1928.* New York: The Macmillan Company, 1930.
Smith, J. Allen. *The Spirit of American Government: A Study of the Constitution: Its Origin, Influence and Relation to Democracy.* New York: The Macmillan Company, 1912.
Stearns, Harold. *America and the Young Intellectual.* New York: George H. Doran Company, 1921.
Steffens, Lincoln. *The Autobiography of Lincoln Steffens.* New York: Harcourt, Brace and Company, 1931.
——. *The Shame of the Cities.* New York: McClure, Phillips & Co., 1904.

Stoner, John E. *S. O. Levinson and the Pact of Paris: A Study in the Techniques of Influence.* Chicago: The University of Chicago Press, 1942.
Strong, Josiah. *Our Country: Its Possible Future and Its Present Crisis.* New York: Baker & Taylor, 1885.
Sumner, Charles. *Works.* Boston: Lee and Shepard, 1873-1883. Volumes I, X, XIII, XIV.
Sumner, William Graham. *Folkways: A Study of the Sociological Importance of Usages, Manners, Customs, Mores, and Morals.* Boston: Ginn and Company, 1906.
———. *War and Other Essays.* New Haven: Yale University Press, 1911.
———. *What Social Classes Owe to Each Other.* New York: Harper & Brothers, 1883.
Tocqueville, Alexis de. *American Institutions.* Seventh Edition. Boston: John Allyn, 1874.
———. *Democracy in America.* American Edition. New York: J. & H. G. Langley, 1843. 2 volumes.
Townsend, H. G. *Philosophical Ideas in the United States.* New York: American Book Company, 1934.
Trevelyan, George Macaulay. *The Life of John Bright.* London: Constable and Company, Ltd., 1925.
Turner, Frederick Jackson. *The Frontier in American History.* New York: Henry Holt & Company, 1921.
Villard, Oswald Garrison. *Fighting Years: Memoirs of a Liberal Editor.* New York: Harcourt, Brace and Company, 1939.
Walker, Amasa. *The Science of Wealth.* Philadelphia: J. B. Lippincott & Co., 1872.
Ware, Norman J. *The Labor Movement in the United States, 1860-1895.* New York: D. Appleton & Company, 1929.
Weyl, Walter E. *The New Democracy: An Essay on Certain Political and Economic Tendencies in the United States.* New York: The Macmillan Company, 1912.
White, William Allen. *The Autobiography of William Allen White.* New York: The Macmillan Company, 1946.
———. *A Puritan in Babylon: The Story of Calvin Coolidge.* New York: The Macmillan Company, 1938.
Whitman, Walt. *The Complete Writings of Walt Whitman.* Camden Edition. New York: G. P. Putnam's Sons, 1902. 3 volumes.
Wilson, Woodrow. *The New Freedom: A Call for the Emancipation of the Generous Energies of a People.* New York: Doubleday, Page & Company, 1921.
Wish, Harvey. *Contemporary America.* New York: Harper & Brothers Publishers, 1945.

ARTICLES AND SPEECHES

Adamic, Louis. "The Collapse of Organized Labor," *Harper's Magazine*, CLXIV (January, 1932), 178.
Beveridge, Albert J. "The March of the Flag," *Modern Eloquence.* Edited by Thomas B. Reed. Philadelphia: John D. Morris and Company, 1900. Vol. XI, pp. 224-243.

———. "The Republic that Never Retreats," *Modern Eloquence*. Edited by Thomas B. Reed. Philadelphia: John D. Morris and Company, 1900. Vol. I, pp. 70-72.

Calkins, Earnest Elmo. "Business the Civilizer," *Atlantic Monthly*, CXLI (February, 1928), 157.

Godkin, Edwin Lawrence. "Aristocratic Opinions of Democracy," *North American Review*, C (1865), 194-202.

———. "The Economic Man," *North American Review*, CLIII (1891), 491-503.

———. "Democratic Tendencies," *Atlantic Monthly*, LXXIX (1897), 145-161.

Harrington, Fred H. "The Anti-Imperialist Movement in the United States, 1898-1900," *The Mississippi Valley Historical Review*, XXII (1935), 211-230.

Niebuhr, Reinhold. "Catastrophe or Social Control?" *Harper's Magazine*, CLXV (1932), 118.

INDEX

Adams, Charles Francis, Jr., 39, 42, 54, 75
Adams, Herbert Baxter, 20
Adams, John, 36
American Economic Association, 21
American Federation of Labor, 13
Anti-Imperialist League, 75
Anti-trust legislation, 29, 51, 98-99
Arbitration, 71, 79, 80
Arnold, Mathew, 39
Arnold, Thurman, vi (fn 6)
Australian ballot, 50

Bancroft, George, 14, 58
Beard, Charles A., 61, 62
Beecher, Henry Ward, 5, 6
Bellamy, Edward, 22, 23, 24, 26
Beveridge, Albert J., 56, 73, 74
Blair Bill, 10
Boer War, 71
Borah, Senator William E., 89, 100
Brandeis, Louis, 68
Brewer, Justice David, 28, 29, 53
Bright, John, 3
Bryan, William Jennings, 13, 34, 37, 43, 57
Bryant, William Cullen, 14
Bryce, James, vi, 39, 44, 45
Business ethics, 62-63
Butler, Ben, 11, 12, 28

Carey, Henry C., 18, 19, 20
Carnegie, Andrew, 13, 17, 55, 75, 76
Carlyle, Thomas, 39
Chase, Stuart, vi
Child labor laws, 68
Chromo-Civilization, 43
Civil liberties, 121
Civil rights, 5, 10, 11, 12
Civil service, 45-46, 52, 54
Clark, John Bates, 20, 21
Clay, Henry, 18, 19
Clayton Act, 68
Cleveland, Grover
  imperialism, 75, 78
  reform, 46, 52, 55, 57
  tariff, 26-27, 43
Cobden, Richard, 71
Cohen, Morris R., 109
Communism, 94
Conscription, 83, 84, 85
Coolidge, Calvin, 97, 105, 107, 109

Corrupt practices legislation, 50, 54
Court of Arbitration, 79
Croly, Herbert, 64, 65, 66, 69
Curtis, George William, 4, 13, 45

Dana, Richard Henry, Jr., vi, 3, 7
Davis, Elmer, 109
Debs, Eugene, 57, 97, 100, 120
Denslow, Van Buren, 20
Dewey, John, 89, 93, 109, 115
Dicey, Albert, vi, 71
Direct election of senators, 68
Direct primary, 50, 68
Disarmament, 73, 80, 85, 86, 89, 90, 92

Economic interpretation of history, 62
Eight-hour day, 31, 32
Elective judiciary, 38, 51
Ely, Richard T., 15, 20, 21, 22
Ernst, Morris L., 109
Ethical economists, 20-22
Executive budget, 47

Fascism, 90
Federal Trade Commission, 68, 99
Field, David Dudley, vii, 14
Field, Stephen J., 53
Fuller, Harold de Wolf, viii, ix, 83

Garrison, Wendell Phillips, vii, viii
Garrison, William Lloyd, 4
George, Henry, 12, 22, 23, 24
Godkin, Edwin Lawrence, vii-ix, 3
  Civil War, 4
  civil service reform, 45-46
  democracy, 41-42, 44, 52, 55
  imperialism, 71-72, 75, 77
  liberalism, 111-112, 117, 119, 120
  Negro suffrage, 7-8, 121
  political economy, 17
Godwin, Parke, 6
Gompers, Samuel, 13, 85
Gould, Jay, 37, 42, 51
Greeley, Horace, 19, 20
Greenback-ism, 13, 34, 38

Hague Conference, 79-80
Hamilton, Alexander, 18, 57, 95, 97, 106
Hanna, Mark, 37, 43
Harding, Warren G., 95, 96, 97, 107
Hitler, Adolf, 91, 92
Hoar, Senator George F., 75

INDEX

Hobhouse, L. T., 115
Hoover, Herbert, 96, 97, 103, 105-109
Hughes, Charles Evans, 82
Humphrey, William E., 98-99

Imperialism, 71-78, 80, 87, 90, 92, 119
Income tax, 51, 68
Initiative, 67, 68
Injunction, 51
International Court, 85
Interstate Commerce Commission, 68, 99
Isolation, 73, 84, 87
Item veto, 47

James, E. J., 20
James, William, viii
Joad, C. E. M., 116
Jordan, David Starr, 75, 77

Kelley, William D., 12, 19, 20
Kellogg-Briand Pact, 88, 90
Kirchwey, Freda, vi
Knights of Labor, 13, 21, 29
Krutch, Joseph Wood, 95

Labor, 18-19, 21-22, 31, 35
LaFollette, Senator Robert, 82, 83, 100, 101
Laidler, Harry W., 103
Laissez-faire, 12-18, 45, 62, 71, 79, 93, 95-97, 99, 104, 112-113, 115
Lamont, Hammond, viii, ix
Laski, Harold, vi
League of Nations, 85, 86-87, 89, 90, 121
Lecky, William Edward, 37, 39, 40, 44, 54
Leggett, William, 14
Legislative reform, 48-49, 50
Lerner, Max, 61
Levinson, S. O., 88-89
Lieber, Francis, vi, 14
Lincoln, Abraham, 26
Lippincott, Benjamin, 39, 54
Lippmann, Walter, 64, 69, 95
List, Frederick, 18
Lloyd, Henry Demarest, 55
Locarno Treaty, 88, 90
Lodge, Senator Henry Cabot, 85
Lowell, James Russell, vi, 4, 51, 112
   civil service, 45
   democracy, 36, 37, 38, 52
   Negro suffrage, 5, 7, 9
   political economy, 17, 35

McKim, James Miller, vii
McKinley, William, 34, 43, 73
McNary-Haugen Bill, 102
Madison, James, 57, 61
Mahan, Alfred T., 73, 81
Maine, Henry Sumner, 39, 40, 54

Malthusian theory, 23, 119
Marx, Karl, 26, 28, 58
Mazur, Paul M., 105
Mellon, Andrew, 97
More, Paul Elmer, viii, ix, 69 (fn 64)
Mill, John Stuart, 55, 74, 112
   Civil War, 3
   democracy, 44
   Negro suffrage, 6-7
   political economy, 13, 20, 24, 105
   woman's suffrage, 50 (fn 69)
Morison, Samuel Eliot, 106
Morrison, Charles Clayton, 89
Mussolini, Benito, 90, 91, 92, 107
Myers, Gustavus, 62

Natural rights, 112-115
Negro, 5-12, 38, 68, 121
Neutrality, 81-83
"New Freedom," 67
Niebuhr, Reinhold, 109
Norris, George W., 96
Norton, Charles Eliot, vii, 17, 51
   democracy, 36-37
   imperialism, 75-76, 77
   Negro suffrage, 7-8, 9

Ogden, Rollo, viii
Outlawry of war, 88-89

Pacifism, 84-87, 120-121
Panama Canal, 78
Parker, John M., 51, 57
Patten, Simon, 20, 21
Perry, Arthur L., 16, 22
Phillips, David Graham, 62
Phillips, Wendell, 7, 35, 42, 52
Populism, 13, 33
Powderly, Terrence V., 13, 30, 37, 57
Powell, Thomas R., 85
President, eligibility of, 47
Progressivism, 93, 99-102

Railroad regulation, 22, 27, 28, 38, 68
Raymond, Daniel, 14
Recall, 67, 68
Reconstruction, 5-7, 9-11, 40, 93
Reconstruction Finance Corporation, 108
Referendum, 50, 67, 68
Ricardo, David, 13, 105
Roosevelt, Franklin D., 109, 110
Roosevelt, Theodore, vi, 47, 57, 66, 67, 68, 85
Root, Elihu, 93
Ruskin, John, 39
Russian Revolution, 91

Schurz, Carl, 7, 9, 36, 45, 51, 75, 76, 77
Sedgwick, Theodore, Jr., 14
Seligman, E. R. A., 20

Shaw, George Bernard, 99
Sherman Silver Purchase Act, 34
Shotwell, James T., 87, 89
Siegfried, André, 104, 106
Slavery, 3, 112
Smoot-Hawley Tariff, 108
Smith, Adam, 13, 14, 35, 105
Smith, Alfred E., 103
Smith, J. Allen, 59, 60, 61, 62, 63
Social Darwinism, 23
Socialism, 24, 25, 94
Sovereignty, 5
Spanish-American War, 71, 73, 76, 78, 119
Spencer, Herbert, 17, 42
Stimson Non-Recognition Doctrine, 88
Stone, I. F., 120
Stearns, Harold, 94
Steffens, Lincoln, 62, 105, 107
Stephen, Leslie, 37, 39, 40
Steward, Ira, 32
Strong, Josiah, 72, 73
Suffrage
  Negro, 5-12, 49, 118
  women, 38, 49, 118
Sumner, Charles, 6, 7, 74, 88, 89
Sumner, William Graham, vi, 16, 33, 75, 77
Survival of the fittest, 72-73, 74, 77

Taft, William Howard, 57, 67, 98
Tarbell, Ida 62
Tariff, 18, 19, 25, 26, 38, 108
Thomas, Norman, 103, 109
Tocqueville, Alexis de, 38, 44, 53, 114

Trade unionism, 29-31
Treaty of Versailles, 87
Trusts, 68
Turner, Frederick Jackson, 58, 62
Tweed, 'Boss,' 11, 12, 37, 41, 51

Unemployment, 108
Utilitarianism, 112-116, 119, 120

Veblen, Thorstein, 58-59, 62
Villard, Henry, viii
Villard, Oswald Garrison, viii, ix, 109, 117
  peace program, 85-86, 88, 89, 120, 121
  progressivism, 93-94, 100, 111
  Russian Revolution, 91
  Spanish-American War, 78
  World War I, 83-84

Wage-fund theory, 30, 31, 33
Walker, Francis Amasa, 16, 22
Wayland, Francis, 15
Weyl, Walter, 63, 64, 69, 115
Wheeler, Burton K., 100
White, Horace, viii
White, William Allen, 67, 97, 98, 99
Whitman, Walt, 36
Wilson, Woodrow, 89
  League of Nations, 86, 87
  New Freedom, 66, 67, 116
  World War I, 82-84
Wood, Fernando, 11
World Court, 89, 90
World War I, 81-84
Wright, Quincy, 88

THE JAMES SPRUNT STUDIES IN HISTORY AND POLITICAL SCIENCE

No. 1. PERSONNEL OF THE CONVENTION OF 1861. By John Gilchrist McCormick
LEGISLATION OF THE CONVENTION OF 1861. By Kemp P. Battle. } (Out of print.)

No. 2. THE CONGRESSIONAL CAREER OF NATHANIEL MACON. By Edwin Mood Wilson. (Out of print.)

No. 3. THE LETTERS OF NATHANIEL MACON, JOHN STEELE, AND WILLIAM BARRY GROVE, WITH NOTES. By Kemp P. Battle. (Out of print.)

No. 4. LETTERS AND DOCUMENTS RELATING TO THE EARLY HISTORY OF THE LOWER CAPE FEAR, WITH INTRODUCTION AND NOTES. By Kemp P. Battle. (Out of print.)

No. 5. MINUTES OF THE KEHUKEY ASSOCIATION, WITH INTRODUCTION AND NOTES. By Kemp P. Battle. (Out of print.)

No. 6. DIARY OF A GEOLOGICAL TOUR BY ELISHA MITCHELL IN 1827 AND 1828, WITH INTRODUCTION AND NOTES. By Kemp P. Battle.

No. 7. WILLIAM RICHARDSON DAVIE: A MEMOIR. By J. G. de Roulhac Hamilton.
LETTERS OF WILLIAM RICHARDSON DAVIE, WITH NOTES. By Kemp P. Battle.

No. 8. THE PROVINCIAL COUNCIL AND COMMITTEES OF SAFETY IN NORTH CAROLINA. By Bessie Lewis Whitaker.

VOL. 9, No. 1. THE SOCIETY FOR THE PROPAGATION OF THE GOSPEL IN THE PROVINCE OF NORTH CAROLINA. By D. D. Oliver.
CORRESPONDENCE OF JOHN RUST EATON. Edited by J. G. de Roulhac Hamilton.

VOL. 9, No. 2. FEDERALISM IN NORTH CAROLINA. By Henry M. Wagstaff.
LETTERS OF WILLIAM BARRY GROVE. Edited by Henry M. Wagstaff.

VOL. 10, No. 1. BENJAMIN SHERWOOD HEDRICK. By J. G. de Roulhac Hamilton.

VOL. 10, No. 2. BARTLETT YANCEY. By George A. Anderson.
THE POLITICAL AND PROFESSIONAL CAREER OF BARTLETT YANCEY. By J. G. de Roulhac Hamilton.
LETTERS TO BARTLETT YANCEY.

VOL. 11, No. 1. COUNTY GOVERNMENT IN COLONIAL NORTH CAROLINA. By W. C. Guess.

VOL. 11, No. 2. THE NORTH CAROLINA CONSTITUTION OF 1776, AND ITS MAKERS. By Frank Nash.
THE GERMAN SETTLERS OF LINCOLN COUNTY AND WESTERN NORTH CAROLINA. By Joseph R. Nixon.

VOL. 12, No. 1. THE GOVERNOR, COUNCIL, AND ASSEMBLY IN ROYAL NORTH CAROLINA. By C. S. Cooke.
LAND TENURE IN PROPRIETARY NORTH CAROLINA. By L. N. Morgan.

VOL. 12, No. 2. THE NORTH CAROLINA INDIANS. By James Hall Rand.

VOL. 13, No. 1. THE GRANVILLE DISTRICT. By E. Merton Coulter.
THE NORTH CAROLINA COLONIAL BAR. By E. H. Alderman.

VOL. 13, No. 2. THE HARRINGTON LETTERS. Edited by H. M. Wagstaff.

VOL. 14, No. 1. THE HARRIS LETTERS. Edited by H. M. Wagstaff.

VOL. 14, No. 2. SOME COLONIAL HISTORY OF BEAUFORT COUNTY. By F. H. Cooper.

VOL. 15, Nos. 1 and 2. PARTY POLITICS IN NORTH CAROLINA, 1835-1860. By J. G. de Roulhac Hamilton.

VOL. 16, No. 1. A COLONIAL HISTORY OF ROWAN COUNTY, NORTH CAROLINA. By S. J. Ervin. (Out of print.)

VOL. 16, No. 2. THE DIARY OF BARTLETT YANCEY MALONE. Edited by Wm. Whatley Pierson, Jr.
THE PROVINCIAL AGENTS OF NORTH CAROLINA. By Samuel James Ervin, Jr.

VOL. 17, No. 1. THE FREE NEGRO IN NORTH CAROLINA. By R. H. Taylor.
SOME COLONIAL HISTORY OF CRAVEN COUNTY, NORTH CAROLINA. By Francis H. Cooper.

VOL. 17, No. 2. JOURNAL OF A TOUR OF NORTH CAROLINA BY WILLIAM ATTMORE, 1787. Edited by Lida Tunstall Rodman.

VOL. 18, Nos. 1 and 2. SLAVEHOLDING IN NORTH CAROLINA: AN ECONOMIC VIEW. By Rosser Howard Taylor.

VOL. 19, No. 1. PRESENT STATUS OF MODERN EUROPEAN HISTORY IN THE UNITED STATES. By Chester Penn Higby.

THE JAMES SPRUNT STUDIES IN HISTORY AND POLITICAL SCIENCE

(Continued from inside front cover)

VOL. 19, No. 2. STUDIES IN HISPANIC-AMERICAN HISTORY. Edited by W. W. Pierson, Jr.

VOL. 20, No. 1. NORTH CAROLINA NEWSPAPERS BEFORE 1790. By Charles Christopher Crittenden.

VOL. 20, No. 2. THE JAMES A. GRAHAM PAPERS, 1861-1884. Edited by H. M. Wagstaff.

VOL. 21, Nos. 1 and 2. THE DEMOCRATIC PARTY IN ANTE-BELLUM NORTH CAROLINA, 1835-1861. By Clarence Clifford Norton.

VOL. 22, Nos. 1 and 2. MINUTES OF THE NORTH CAROLINA MANUMISSION SOCIETY, 1816-1834. Edited by H. M. Wagstaff.

VOL. 23, No. 1. THE PRESIDENTIAL ELECTION OF 1824 IN NORTH CAROLINA. By Albert Ray Newsome.

VOL. 23, No. 2. THE SECESSION MOVEMENT IN NORTH CAROLINA. By Joseph Carlyle Sitterson.

VOL. 24, No. 1. JEFFERSONIAN DEMOCRACY IN SOUTH CAROLINA. By John Harold Wolfe.

VOL. 24, No. 2. GUIDE TO THE MANUSCRIPTS IN THE SOUTHERN HISTORICAL COLLECTION OF THE UNIVERSITY OF NORTH CAROLINA.

VOL. 25, No. 1. NORTH CAROLINA BOUNDARY DISPUTES INVOLVING HER SOUTHERN LINE. By Marvin L. Skaggs.

VOL. 25, No. 2. ANTE-BELLUM SOUTH CAROLINA: A SOCIAL AND CULTURAL HISTORY. By Rosser H. Taylor.

VOL. 26, No. 1. THE PROHIBITION MOVEMENT IN ALABAMA, 1702 TO 1943. By James Benson Sellers.

VOLUME 27. PROHIBITION IN NORTH CAROLINA, 1715-1945. By Daniel Jay Whitener.

VOLUME 28. THE NEGRO IN MISSISSIPPI, 1865-1890. By Vernon Lane Wharton.

VOLUME 29. THE WHIG PARTY IN GEORGIA, 1825-1853. By Paul Murray.

VOLUME 30. THE SOUTH IN ACTION: A SECTIONAL CRUSADE AGAINST FREIGHT RATE DISCRIMINATION. By Robert A. Lively.

VOLUME 31. ESSAYS IN SOUTHERN HISTORY. Edited by Fletcher Melvin Green.

VOLUME 32. SOUTH CAROLINA GOES TO WAR. By Charles Edward Cauthen.

VOLUME 33. REVOLUTIONARY JUSTICE: A STUDY OF THE ORGANIZATION, PERSONNEL, AND PROCEDURE OF THE PARIS TRIBUNAL, 1793-1795. By James Logan Godfrey.

VOLUME 34. THE POLITICAL LIBERALISM OF THE NEW YORK *Nation*, 1865-1932. BY Alan Pendleton Grimes.

www.ingramcontent.com/pod-product-compliance
Lightning Source LLC
Chambersburg PA
CBHW030115010526
44116CB00005B/262